A Short Guide to Writing a Thesis

ACU Series

1. *Faith and Reason*, 2004 edited by Anthony Fisher OP and Hayden Ramsay.

A Short Guide to Writing a Thesis

What to do and what not to do

by

Gerald O'Collins, SJ

Adelaide
2011

Text copyright © 2011 remains with the author.

All rights reserved. Except for any fair dealing permitted under the Copyright Act, no part of this book may be reproduced by any means without prior permission. Inquiries should be made to the publisher.

National Library of Australia Cataloguing-in-Publication entry (pbk)

Author: O'Collins, Gerald, 1931-

Title: A short guide to writing a thesis : what to do and what not to do / Gerald Glynn O'Collins.

ISBN: 9781921511141 (pdf.)

Notes: Includes bibliographical references.

Subjects: Dissertations, Academic--Style manuals.
            Authorship--Style manuals.

Dewey Number: 808.066378

National Library of Australia Cataloguing-in-Publication entry (eBook)

Author: O'Collins, Gerald, 1931-

Cover and layout design by Astrid Sengkey

An imprint of the ATF Ltd
PO Box 504
Hindmarsh, SA 5007
ABN 90 116 359 963
www.atfpress.com

Preface

Having examined nearly two thousand substantial essays or term papers, supervised to a successful conclusion over two hundred master's theses and nearly one hundred doctoral dissertations, and examined over one hundred further doctoral dissertations, I have come to realise that I could pass on some street wisdom for those doing research in the humanities and the social sciences. From all that supervising and examining I have picked up a good number of ideas about writing essays and theses—about the things students should do and not do.

How might they choose a topic that they can investigate and turn into a short paper or a long dissertation? What should feed into their choice of a supervisor? How should they compile and organise their bibliography and set about writing the introduction? What are some tips for writing paragraphs and entire chapters and producing conclusions? What are ways of providing references, using helpful (or at least correct) punctuation, avoiding common mistakes in spelling, and improving their level of writing? When difficulties arise—for instance, with their supervisor—how might they cope with and resolve such difficulties?

Frequently presenting a dissertation and even a term paper at the honor's level involves some kind of face-to-face meeting with examiners. How might students prepare themselves for these oral examinations and perform more successfully? What suggestions can I offer for those who want or need to publish their theses in part or perhaps even in whole?

Research students in the English-speaking world already use such admirable works as Joseph Gibaldi's *MLA [Modern Language*

Association] Handbook for Writers of Research Papers and the latest edition of Kate Turabian's *A Manual for Writers of Term Papers, Theses and Dissertations*. But such books are much longer than the short guide I am offering. At times they go into detail about minor questions and occasionally seem to lack a fully practical edge. Postgraduate (also called graduate) students, as well as undergraduates, need clear advice about issues and problems that I have seen repeatedly occur over the years. How can they improve their style of writing? What can be done when difficulties arise with their dissertation or with their supervisor?

This guide offers some straightforward suggestions about doing research, putting the results into a convincing form, and dealing with difficulties that inevitably arise. The overall objective of this work is to provide students and their supervisors with some down-to-earth proposals about things to do and things to avoid when preparing and producing a long essay or a thesis.

I am very grateful to John Begley, Stephen Connelly, Anne Hunt, Catherine Playoust, Michael Smith, and Bill Uren for help, support and suggestions. I dedicate this work to the Australian Catholic University, who appointed me an adjunct professor and have now awarded me an honorary doctorate.

Australian Catholic University, Melbourne	Gerald O'Collins, SJ 16 June 2010.

Contents

Preface	3
Chapter One: Choosing a Supervisor and a Topic	7
Chapter Two: Organising the Bibliography and Writing the Introduction	17
Chapter Three: The Personal Touch	31
Chapter Four: Writing Elegant Chapters, Paragraphs, and Footnotes	35
Chapter Five: Words, Spelling, and Punctuation	47
Chapter Six: Some Don'ts, Do's, and Possibilities	57
Chapter Seven: Defending and Publishing the Thesis	63
Epilogue: On Supervising Theses	69
Select Bibliography	75
A Guide Sheet	77
Index	81

Chapter One
Choosing a Supervisor and a Topic

Students who need to write long essays or end-of-term papers often have only a limited choice of topics. Their lecturer or tutor prescribes a particular theme or a small list of possible themes, and that is that. The students may have been free in choosing the course (with its lecturer or the tutor). But, once enrolled for a course or a seminar, they will find that the topics for essays or seminar/tutorial papers will often be, more or less, prescribed.

Choosing a Supervisor

For those pursuing a master's or doctoral degree, important decisions come into play. At which college or university should I do (or can I do) my research and writing? What professor or lecturer should I approach with a view to finding a satisfactory PhD supervisor or dissertation director? Unquestionably, previous experience of a particular department, the availability of research grants, the possibility of being supervised by a leading figure in my chosen field, and a wide range of personal circumstances can affect my decision. Some institutions simply assign supervisors to those students admitted to begin research. But what of those students who enjoy some freedom in settling their thesis director?

They may recognise that several professors or lecturers could make suitable directors. Such possible directors could be younger and on the way up or older and heading toward retirement. The prospect of being supervised by someone who is already an acknowledged leader in his or her field and even a world-ranking specialist can be attractive. Yet students may sometimes be helped more effectively by a younger, promising academic, who has the time and energy to follow their students' research closely and provide pertinent suggestions and criticisms. In general, supervisors who are regularly available and ready to comment quickly on the work in progress are to be preferred to celebrities who take many weeks to read their students' chapters and then have very few criticisms and corrections to offer. Here those students who are completing or have recently completed dissertations in one's department or faculty can, out of their own experience, give good advice about the comparative merits of supervisors.

Some possible supervisors gather their research students for monthly or even weekly seminar sessions, at which the students present the results of their work. The chance of profiting from such feedback may be a significant item to weigh in deciding on one's supervisor.

Dealing over many years with students hesitant about their choice of supervisor, I normally suggested sending a letter to possible supervisors, in which the students gave a brief 'curriculum vitae' (along with their address and contact information), indicated their general area of research, and mentioned that they would be phoning or e-mailing shortly to ask for an appointment. I also suggested that they should add that they were simply seeking some direction about their choice of research topic and supervisor and were not formally asking the professor in question to be their supervisor. Such letters constantly brought the students four major benefits. First, they saved time, as the students did not need to go into details about their previous work, personal circumstances, and area of research when they came for the appointment. The professor or lecturer already knew all that in advance. Second, the person they approached had the time to reflect on possible advice and even write up some useful questions and references. Third, taking time to compose such a letter showed an attractive seriousness of purpose and genuine respect for the professor or lecturer they had contacted. While writing such a letter in the past constantly proved an investment that brought good dividends, in the new age of e-mails such a letter arriving by post can prove even more impressive and useful. Fourth, such an advance letter could take any undesirable pressure out of the meeting. The students were seeking for help and advice from an expert, and not necessarily asking the expert in question to become their supervisor.

Whether it happens quickly or more slowly, the choice of a supervisor for one's research is a momentous decision that represents a quantum leap in the life of students. Previously, when following various courses and attending different seminars, their academic and personal wellbeing did not depend on smooth and fruitful relations with only one person. They dealt, happily or less happily, with a series of teachers. Choosing or accepting a dissertation director means entrusting their present prospects and future advancement to just one person. Academically and psychologically this is a major, new step for them. I sometimes told research students, especially those taking on a doctoral director, that they were entering a personal relationship that was a kind of marriage. Their 'spouse' could make or break the course of their academic lives. Normally without indulging such dramatic talk, I would warn them: 'your director may not always help you in doing your research and writing your dissertation as much as you might expect. Just as happens in many marriages, there will be ups and downs and unfulfilled expectations. Both of you will need understanding and encouragement toward seeing the long task through to a happy conclusion.'

When giving such advice, I usually did not add that a few dissertation directors I had known have acted in ways that should be branded as unacceptable and even downright unjust. They could airily encourage students to 'take their time and spend a year or more reading around the topic'. That kind of advice easily ignores the need for students to move ahead briskly. Their financial resources often do not allow them the luxury of months or even years of leisurely reading. Academically they would be well advised to finish and defend their dissertation in a reasonably short amount of time, so that, now armed with a PhD, they can apply for positions at colleges or universities. Then, some supervisors take an inordinate amount of time to read the chapters their students submit to them. This can cause students distressing unease about the way their research is moving ahead. At times the chapters are eventually returned with only a few comments and suggestions. Students may wonder whether their supervisor has given their work serious attention. All in all, every now and then I have been left wondering whether some dissertation directors are sufficiently sensitive to the personal, financial, and academic wellbeing of their students. This could happen with supervisors who take on too many students and too much outside work, and finish up failing to meet their students regularly and to give them the amount of attention and help that is needed.

Dealing at once with work that students present characterises first rate supervisors. It always strikes me as odd that some supervisors take weeks in reviewing and evaluating the work presented by their research students. They are going to do the reviewing and evaluating anyway. Why not do all that at once and give their students the vivid encouragement that comes from a quick and thoughtful reply?

In some academic institutions students may have more than one research supervisor. Provided the supervisors in question enjoy a reasonable working relationship and do not insist one-sidedly on a personal method and point of view, so that students feel themselves to be caught like the children of a dysfunctional marriage, multiple supervision offers considerable advantages—not least that students can profit from more intelligent comment. In general, one should say that the more feedback, the better.

Choosing a Theme

Let me offer twelve suggestions about choosing a theme for research.

(1) Some fortunate students, when they arrive at the level of a master's or a doctoral degree, find or are given a very well informed supervisor who suggests to them one or more fruitful themes for research—projects that he or she knows will work, without having the time personally to pursue them. Others students come to research with a clearly profiled theme they want to investigate. This theme may have emerged even years before—for instance, in the course of

their work on an undergraduate essay or paper. Or else something they once heard in a course or seminar or read in a book might have roused their curiosity and ongoing interest.

Someone in a literature course could, for example, have alerted them to the topic of midlife journeys in fiction. The power of youth is gone, the possibility of failure presents itself, and the dreams of earlier years turn out to be shallow or even pointless. This is the crisis of the middle years, a midlife journey that we find, for instance, in Herman Hesse's *Siddhartha*, Doris Lessing's *The Summer Before the Dark*, and Patrick White's *Riders in the Chariot, The Tree of Man*, and *Voss*. Such works presents middle-aged men or women caught up in strange adventures and walking unexpected roads. A research thesis in literature could profitably investigate the theme of midlife journeys in the novels of White or else compare and contrast how some major authors have dealt with this theme.

(2) But many students come to research with a sense of their general area but without having formulated yet the precise issue they will take up. Besides engaging in discussion with possible supervisors, they can help themselves choose their topic by checking the titles and abstracts of theses in their area (e.g. in anthropology, education, fine arts, history, languages, law, literature, or psychology) that have been successfully presented in recent years. Such information can be available in printed form or on line. The research that others have been doing can readily suggest similar but new themes to be pursued.

(3) Insights into valuable topics for research could also be prompted by browsing through journals in one's area, or reading them on online. The articles, news and reviews that appear, for instance, in such journals as *British Journal of Sociology, The Burlington Magazine, History Today,* and *The Journal of Philosophy* reflect many issues that teachers and researchers in sociology, fine arts, history and philosophy, respectively, have been currently investigating and the kind of work that merits study and publication.

(4) A fourth avenue towards the choice of a dissertation topic can open up by reading entries in first-rate, contemporary dictionaries and encyclopedias. In philosophy, for instance, perusing some of the entries in the *Encyclopedia of Philosophy*[1], *Routledge Encyclopedia of Philosophy*[2], and the *Stanford Encyclopedia of Philosophy* (online) can bring happy results. Some of their entries, along with the bibliographies, may easily suggest fresh lines for research.

(5) For those engaged in historical and literary research, trawling through archives might bring to light some unpublished material that would make a valuable subject for research and publication. When the letters, diaries, and unpublished work of some notable people become available, a scholarly edition of at least a part of such papers, with a substantial and appropriate introduction based on the necessary research, could be a welcome contribution. Obviously one should recall here the fresh possibilities for those doing research in economics and political science, when government archives open up decades of hitherto embargoed documents.

(6) In one's own city or country, the life and work of recently deceased leaders in education, finance, industry, politics, religion and sport offer interesting possibilities for research in such areas as commerce, education, history, political science and religious studies. Initial contacts with the institutions for which the deceased worked and with their family and friends will show whether it is feasible to select one such outstanding figures as a dissertation topic. Similarly, research students could select a period in the story of some corporation, political party, religious body or other such association. These groups might well provide much help for students engaged in examining their history.

(7) Whatever way students go in finding a thesis topic, input from others is normally essential. Many years ago one professor said to me when I was starting my own doctoral research at the University of Cambridge: 'A theme will come to you some morning when you are looking in the mirror and shaving.' This advice ignored the way

---

1. DM Borchert (ed), *Encyclopedia of Philosophy*, 10 vols (2nd edn; Farmington Hills, Mich: Macmillan, 2006).
2. E Craig (ed), *Routledge Encyclopedia of Philosophy*, 10 vols (London: Routledge, 1998).

in which fresh knowledge and insight come through contact with others, their interests, and their research. Later I recognised that, without realising it, he had revealed what he himself did. After landing on a 'bright idea', often an idiosyncratic conviction, he then set himself to 'prove' it in an article or a book. There should, of course, be something new about the theme chosen for research—at least at the doctoral level. But the knowledge needed for making such a choice is not normally given by 'inspiration from heaven' coming in front of a mirror but emerges through dialogue with others.

(8) The theme chosen should have its clearly defined limits and keep to a precise minimum. Dissertations in the humanities often involve studying a very specific issue or some particular writer at depth, or sometimes both, as when a student investigates X's idea of Y. Inevitably great authors have already generated a great deal of comment and interpretation. Research students in literature will can hardly expect to identify some new line to develop in examining and commenting directly on Dante's *Divine Comedy*, Shakespeare's sonnets, Milton's *Paradise Lost*, William Faulkner's novels, TS Eliot's *Four Quartets*, or the plays of Eugene O'Neill and Tennessee Williams. Yet, even in the case of major authors in literature, philosophy, or theology, there might still be a serious question or area that has so far escaped attention. Some years ago I examined an excellent dissertation on John Henry Newman's eschatology or teaching on 'the last things' to be expected in human history or in the history of individuals. Despite the massive secondary literature that had gathered around him through the twentieth century, no student had so far tackled his eschatology—at least from a theological point of view.

The way great authors have been received and interpreted in another part of the world yields some possible topics for dissertation. How, for example, have the novels of Shusaku Endo or the poetry of Rabindranath Tagore been received in the British Isles and North America? What reception have the plays of Shakespeare enjoyed in Japan, Korea or Singapore during a certain period (eg from 1945 to date)?

(9) The difficulty in finding authors who have not provoked much comment may be avoided by doing research into some important but secondary figure in the history, for instance, of education, law, literature, philosophy, or theology. Almost inevitably such writers will not prove as exciting as the major figures. Yet students will be delivered from the task of reading much secondary comment. They can do something clearly new, through becoming 'the' expert on this or that relatively minor writer.

(10) There are, however, at least two ways of doing acceptable doctoral work on central and much studied authors. Students can select a particular question and see how it was handled by three or four mainline thinkers. Normally, such a group should be selected on grounds that bring them together into a plausible 'team': they lived in the same century; they were in dialogue or debate with each other; they faced the same issues or made contributions in the same field. In philosophy one could imagine a thesis that critically presented a team of three or four major writers who in the first or second half of the twentieth century took up what David Hume had written on miracles. Such a thesis would enjoy two major advantages: it involves a careful study of Hume himself; it also allows the research student to become thoroughly acquainted with several modern philosophers. The thesis should confine itself to comparing and contrasting how these philosophers evaluated Hume's thought. At the same time, researching such a thesis would bring a wider knowledge of Hume and some modern philosophers—a valuable educative process that would accompany the narrower project of composing the thesis itself.

(11) Another possibility entails casting the net somewhat wider by selecting an author who had written a landmark study, for instance, on Shakespeare and then examining where the study of the sonnets had been taken in the twenty or twenty-five years after that study. One could undertake something similar in the case of significant historical or literary figures. A critical and comparative account of works about George Washington, William Gladstone, WB Yeats, Mahatma Gandhi, or Sun Yat-sen—to pull in a few names almost at random--could produce some enlightening and even fas-

cinating conclusions about shifting criteria for evaluating their contributions and about the impact of new data that became available in the aftermath of the first scholarly studies of these figures.

(12) Finally, interviews conducted and assessed with scientific rigour can yield worthwhile results for those doing research in social history. One could imagine some fresh and fascinating conclusions emerging from interviews with scientists now in retirement who moved in a particular decade from the British Isles and continental Europe to the United States. There is surely much research still to be done in examining and evaluating historically samples of such a 'brain-drain'.

Living with the Topic

Over many years of work with research students, I experienced the need to warn them right at the start that, almost inevitably, some crisis would occur sooner or later. It they were forewarned, that made them 'fore-armed' when a serious difficulty arose. Students may become bored with their topic and with slogging away at the research. Financial and personal difficulties can arise. They may come to find their supervisor irritating and unhelpful. After a smooth run through their research, at the end they can meet difficulties that arise from a member of the committee involved with the submission of the dissertation or from one of the board of examiners

Admittedly a minority of research students enjoy peaceful progress--from the start right through to the finish when their dissertation is examined and accepted. But the majority, sooner or later, run up against difficulties. Recognising that this might occur, without lapsing into anxious fears about what might happen in the next few months or years, can take some pain out of awkward situations that arise. Moreover, every college and university has one or more officials to whom they can turn: the head of the department or, even better, someone who oversees research and research students in the whole institution. At times sharing a difficulty more or less solves the difficulty. Students should not suffer in silence. If their supervisor, for whatever reason, fails to provide the needed help, there is always someone else higher up to whom they can turn.

A later chapter in this guide will address other challenges that can or will arise. Let me now suppose that a student has chosen both his or her supervisor and topic, and move next to the task of research and writing.

Chapter Two
Organising the Bibliography and Writing the Introduction

My research students were often surprised when I asked them to begin by gathering and organising their biography and by writing an introduction to their thesis. Many had imagined that they were only gradually to build up the biography while they went ahead with the task of researching and writing their dissertation. How could they tell at the start which books, articles, and unpublished sources might be relevant to their project? Many had also anticipated that they would write the introduction after more or less completing the work. Surely it was only at the end that they could appreciate clearly the work that was to be introduced?

Organising the Bibliography

Putting together a bibliography means organising one's thinking about a theme and placing that theme in the context of current research.[1] Obviously, right at the start of their research, students, by definition, will at best have read only some of the works they list in their bibliography. But a quick browse and/or some indications from those authors they have already read will show, at least provisionally, that certain books and articles are relevant to the project in hand. Subsequent reading will probably confirm this preliminary judgement, or else lead to some entries in the bibliography being discarded. Other items will undoubtedly be added to the bibliog-

---

1. *New Hart's Rules: The Handbook of Style for Writers and Editors* (Oxford: Oxford University Press, 2005), 328–54; this chapter ('Bibliography') ends with directions about websites and other electronic data (350–4).

raphy as the research moves ahead. Any bibliography gathered at the start of one's research will always be somewhat provisional. But preparing such a bibliography helps students to see their project in a fuller context of contemporary research, and to sharpen their vision of the way in which it can be developed and should be limited.

When preparing a bibliography, whether on online or in a library, students should take down all the details – not only the year of publication, publishers, and so forth, but also the shelf numbers in the library. Doing this work thoroughly the first time means never wasting time on looking up such details once again. The students may record the details with their laptop, or else on cards, with one card for each entry. In that way they can swiftly arrange alphabetically the biographical entries. The only 'system' to be avoided is writing down the entries higgledy-piggledy on sheets of paper. That disorderly procedure encourages mistakes and always increases the work load.

Starting with a bibliography also helps students and their supervisor to spot any 'remedial' work that needs to be done at the 'formal' level in constructing bibliographies and the closely related matter of footnotes or endnotes. I used to promise my new research students a bottle of wine if they could prepare a perfect bibliography. But I never needed to make good on my promise. There was always some minor inconsistency or more significant mistakes to be spotted and corrected.

Some bibliographies wavered between *also* noting the publisher of a book (a helpful and preferable practice) and merely indicating the city of publication. Some students seemed unaware of the practice of indicating the state whenever a publisher in the United States is located in a small town: for instance, 'Maryknoll, NY: Orbis Books, 2009'. Or else they took 'NY' to be an abbreviation for the city of New York, and went on to 'sin' against the conventions by writing, for instance, 'NY: Doubleday, 2009'. Or else, since they were expected to write 'Maryknoll, NY' in the case of a book published by Orbis, they wrongly concluded that they should do this with a book published in San Francisco and put down 'San Francisco, CA: HarperSan Francisco'. Since everyone should know that San Francisco is located in the state of California, 'CA' is a useless addition. Some fondly imagined that, since they included the name of the publisher in the case of a book, they should also include the name of the publisher (and, for good measure, the place of publication) for journals. This was to violate the convention of simply supplying the titles of journals and ignoring their place of publication and the name of their publisher. Apropos of journals, some new students were inconsistent in supplying the full title for some journals but inserting an abbreviated title for other journals. At least in the bibliography, they should supply the full titles for all journals.

'Consistency' and 'Convention' were my two battle cries. Some colleges and universities prescribe one way and one way only for doing bibliographies, footnotes (or endnotes), and the title page. In that case consistency requires students to know accurately and observe throughout all the norms of their institution. Other centres, like the Gregorian University (Rome) where I taught for thirty-three years, allowed a variety of systems, since the students came from many parts of the world and normally wanted to follow the system regularly used in their own country: for instance, in Brazil, France, Germany, the United Kingdom, or the United States. But, whatever the system adopted (eg of always providing the name of the publisher or never doing so), the students had to be ruthlessly consistent.

I could pile up examples of sins committed against both (1) *consistency* and (2) *convention*. (1) In the bibliography, as well as in their text or footnotes, a few students would give academic titles to some authors (eg 'Professor' and 'Dr') but not to others. It is preferable never to do this for anyone. In the case of authors who belonged to religious orders, some bibliographies would add 'O.P.' or 'OP' (Order of Preachers or Dominicans) and 'C.Ss.R' (Congregation of the Most Holy Redeemer or Redemptorists) but fail to add 'S.J.' (Society of Jesus) after the name of a Jesuit author. Consistency demands that, if you do this for one author, you should do it for all authors who belong to religious institutes. It seems simpler never to add 'OP' and so forth, and omit all such references after such names in the bibliography and footnotes. Sometimes the abbreviations for states were given with period added (N.Y. and N.J.) and sometimes not (eg NY or NJ). Once again consistency demands using the period for all states (that need to be indicated) or for none (preferable).

Consistency could also be flouted when providing the first names of authors: in an unaccountable way a few students fluctuated between the first initial for some authors (eg G Murray and K Rahner) but the full name for others (eg Maurice Bowra and Rudolf Bultmann). The rule should be either the full names for all authors or the initials for all, but not a mixture. Here, of course, one may need to make exceptions for authors whose first name is widely used (eg Iris Murdoch instead of I Murdoch) or whose initials are widely used and known: for instance, AN Wilson and NT Wright. One should follow the form of the name(s) or initials that individuals are most commonly known by or known to prefer. As regards initials, it seems an unacceptable variation to swing from C.M. Bowra (preferable) to omitting sometimes the periods and writing CM Bowra.

Consistency affects abbreviations that regularly turn up: for instance, 'eds' for editors. One should not waver between this abbreviation and 'eds.' or 'edd' or 'edd.'.

(2) Students should adopt *conventional* abbreviations and avoid creating their own abbreviations. Abbreviations have been long in use for major journals and standard works in various disciplines, and can be easily found. Dictionaries, encyclopedias, and handbooks in different fields frequently provide a long list of such established abbreviations for major journals and some standard works: such abbreviations are provided, for instance, by the *Oxford Dictionary of the Christian Church*.[2]

Titles of books and journals should be underlined or put in italics.[3] But convention does not do this for books of the Bible or for abbreviated titles of these books. One writes Exodus (or Exod. or Exod) but never *Exodus* (or *Exod*). Here too one commonly used

---

2. FL Cross and EA Livingstone (eds), *The Oxford Dictionary of the Christian Church* (3rd edn rev; Oxford: Oxford University Press, 2005).
3. Students may not always know that underlining a title or some other word normally means that, when printed, it will be set in italics.

conventional system for abbreviating the books of the Bible should be adopted and followed throughout.

After those abbreviations that end with the last letter of the word, there is no full stop: for instance, 'dr' (for doctor) and 'dept' (for department). The full stop frequently applies after abbreviations that do not end with the last letter of the word: for instance, 'ed.' (for editor) and 'Rom.' (Paul's Letter to the Romans). But such abbreviations as DPhil or PhD (doctor of philosophy), EEC (European Economic Community) TUC (Trades Union Congress), UFT (United Faculty of Theology) dispense with the full stop in British English. But in such cases American English often prefers to insert periods.

Some systems require that abbreviations for titles should be underlined or italicised: for instance ABD or *ABD* for D. N. Freedman (ed.), *The Anchor Bible Dictionary*, and BJS or *BJS* for the *British Journal of Sociology*. This is not done, however, in the case of abbreviations which refer to the names of editors or authors: for instance, DzH for H. Denzinger and P. Hünermann (eds), *Enchiridion symbolorum, definitionum et declarationum*, and not DzH or *DzH*.

Consistent and Conventional Bibliographies

Consistency and convention should shape the basic system adopted for a bibliography. Titles of books and journals should be either underlined or put in italics; articles in journals, chapters in books, and entries in dictionaries should be listed within quotation marks (or inverted commas). For instance:

Denniston, JD, *The Greek Particles* (2nd edn; Oxford: Oxford University Press, 1954).

Featherby, WJ, 'Revisiting Plato on the Good', *Adelaide Journal of Philosophy*, 16 (2009), 231–66.

Fee, GD, 'Paul and the Metaphors for Salvation: Some Reflections on Pauline Soteriology', in ST Davis, D. Kendall, and G. O'Collins (eds), *The Redemption: An Interdisciplinary Symposium on Christ as Redeemer* (Oxford: Oxford University Press, 2004), 43-67.

Sherry, N., *The Life of Graham Greene*, vol 3 (London: Jonathan Cape, 2004).

Over the years I have known students to sin against this system in a variety of ways.

(1) They can forget to insert the page numbers for an article, something that readers normally want to know. The page range helps readers to locate the article in the journal, as well as indicating the scale (and perhaps significance) of the article.

(2) Committing a kind of 'both belt and braces' mistake, students occasionally put the title of an article *both* in italics and within quotation marks. This doubling up is unnecessary, and in any case I do not know any regularly used system for bibliographies or footnotes that prescribes putting in italics the title of an article.

(3) Another error or at least useless piece of information, so it seems to me, comes from indicating not only the volume number of a journal and its year of publication—for instance, 16 (2009)—but also adding 'winter' or the number of the particular issue within the year: for instance, 16/3(winter 2009). By themselves the volume number and the year already provide all the information necessary for locating the journal on the stacks of a library or on line.

Three Further Remarks on Bibliographies

Before addressing another major system for constructing a bibliography (and for citing works in footnotes or within the text itself), let me add three final remarks on bibliographies. (1) Students should verify for themselves the details of the books, articles, and electronic references included in their bibliographies. Quick Web searches, reading publishers' bulletins, and checking library catalogues (including e-books) do not substitute for personal examination of the articles and books that enter one's bibliography. Some software tools, such as 'EndNote', can help create bibliographies. But students should always verify each entry for themselves.

(2) Bibliographies should contain works that were used in preparing the paper or thesis or at least could be significantly helpful for readers. Hence one should avoid bloated bibliographies that include all manner of works that have at best only a slight connection with the thesis. Discerning examiners appreciate 'lean' bibliogra-

phies that bring together works which have been repeatedly cited in the thesis or which can throw further light on the thesis. This means that, in my view, clearly relevant items may appear in bibliographies, even though they have not been cited in the course of the thesis. This also means that an article or book that has been cited only once in the text need not appear in the bibliography, if it is of only marginal interest. In other words, I doubt the wisdom of insisting that *every* book or article cited the thesis *must also* appear in the bibliography.

(3) Common sense should dictate the *order* and possible *divisions* (or even subdivisions) within the bibliography. Where, let us say, two books by a given author stand at the centre of a thesis, I would recommend that immediately after 'primary sources', which list all the works by this author relevant to the thesis, the 'secondary sources' should begin by listing the major reviews of those two books (or chapters dedicated to them in books). I say, 'major reviews'. Reviews that remain very brief or simply summarise the content of books can be safely ignored. Readers gain nothing by being referred to reviews (or chapters) that prove a waste of their time.

Regular usage prefers an alphabetical order in bibliographies, with the surname of the author or editor coming first. Here students should take care of some foreign names. The 'vons' are not listed under the letter 'v' but as follows: Balthasar, Hans Urs (or HU) von and Harnack, Adolf (or A) von. It is the same with some French names: for instance, Lubac, Henri de. Particular attention should be paid to such cases as Teilhard de Chardin, Pierre (or P); his family name was Teilhard de Chardin, and he should appear under 'T' and not be alphabetised as Chardin or de Chardin.[4] Occasionally some family names may appear to be first names: thus numerous students have been led astray in the case of the Spanish biblical scholar Luis Alonso Schökel. 'Alonso Schökel' was his family name, with 'Luis' as his first name. Hence he should be listed as 'Alonso Schökel, Luis (or L).

---

4. On names containing prefixes, see *New Hart's Rules*, 106-8.

It is only in a very few cases that it may be better to list the authors chronologically and follow the order of the years in which they published. One presumes that an alphabetical order should normally be followed. But, in the case of a dissertation concerned with a particular writer, it would be useful to readers if they could see at a glance the writer's publications in their chronological order.

Likewise, in the case of a dissertation on a specific author, it can help readers if the bibliography is divided into primary and secondary sources, with that author monopolising 'primary sources'. That one division may be enough. Do fussy divisions into 'books', 'articles', 'secondary sources', and 'further reading' really help those reading the thesis and its bibliography?

Finally, unless there are good (and stated) reasons to the contrary, students should use the latest editions of works that have enjoyed more than one edition. Especially in the case of reference books, it creates a bad impression to find some early edition being cited when the work in question has been revised and gone into one or more new editions.

Harvard Referencing Style

These remarks about bibliographies would be outrageously incomplete if I were not to add something about what is known as the 'Harvard Referencing Style' or 'Author-date System', a system for references and bibliographies that has now been adopted or at least accepted well beyond the United States: for instance, at some universities in Australia, Ireland, New Zealand, South Africa, and the United Kingdom. It is found on such websites as 'Harvard System of Referencing Guide', 'Harvard (author-date) style examples', and 'Referencing—the Harvard System'.[5] This system sets out as follows the examples given above:

Featherby, W.J. 2009. Revisiting Plato on the good. *Adelaide Journal of Philosophy*, 16 (4): 231–66.

---

5. See ibid 322-6.

Fee, G.D. 2004. Paul and the metaphors of salvation: some reflections on Pauline soteriology, in *The Redemption: An interdisciplinary Symposium on Christ as redeemer*, edited by S.T. Davis, D. Kendall and G. O'Collins. Oxford: Oxford University Press: 43-67.
Levine, B.A. 2000. *Numbers 21–36*. New York: Doubleday.
O'Collins, G. 2009. *Christology: A biblical, historical, and systematic study of Jesus*. 2nd ed. Oxford: Oxford University Press.

Another, similar system is explained by *The Chicago Manual of Style* and also has its followers outside the United States.[6] In this system the examples I gave above would be set out as follows:

Featherby, W. J. "Revisiting Plato on the Good." *Adelaide Journal of Theology* 16 (2009): 231-66.
Fee, G. D. "Paul and the Metaphors of Salvation: Some Reflections on Pauline Soteriology." In *The Redemption: An Interdisciplinary Symposium on Christ as Redeemer*, edited by S. T. Davis, D. Kendall and G. O'Collins, pp. 43-67. Oxford: Oxford University Press, 2004.
Levine, B. A. *Numbers 21-36*. New York: Doubleday, 2000.
O'Collins, G. *Christology: A Biblical, Historical, and Systematic Study of Jesus*. 2nd ed. Oxford: Oxford University Press, 2009.

Writers often use these two systems or some modification of them when citing or referring to sources in parenthesis—that is to say, within the text itself. One can provide the reference as follows: (Featherby 2009, 242) or, even more simply, when only one publication by Featherby is being cited (Featherby, 242).

Whatever referencing system and whatever format for bibliographies are adopted and however they are modified for good reasons, the cardinal rule is always: consistency must be preserved throughout the dissertation or paper.

---

6. For abundant information on bibliographies, 'mere' reference lists and how they affect footnotes, endnotes, and parenthetical text citation, see *The Chicago Manual of Style*, (15th edn; Chicago and London: The University of Chicago Press, 2003), 593-640

Writing an Introduction

When drafting their introduction, my new students sometimes went astray by starting too 'far back': that is to say, by attempting to summarise in a couple of paragraphs a whole field before coming to the theme of their thesis. I advised them to make a straightforward opening statement about the scope of their work: 'this thesis will investigate X's view of human consciousness'. They could then press on at once to indicate the *sources* they would draw on, the *limits* of what they were attempting, the *method* they would follow, and—in view of the current state of research—the *novelty* of the thesis they propose. They might write:

X developed his view of human consciousness in two books [give their titles and years of publication] and a series of articles published over twenty years. This thesis will, then, not deal either with his approach to ethics or with his occasional articles in the area of the philosophy of science. His two works on human consciousness were widely reviewed. But, as far as I know, we still lack a serious study of his view of consciousness, the reactions to it, and his response to the debate in a second book, which acknowledged certain limits and weaknesses in his first book and added some relevant modifications.

Naturally an introduction needs to indicate the direction the thesis will take and the method that will be adopted:

In an opening chapter I will sketch X's life and philosophical career. Then two chapters will summarise the contents of his two works on human consciousness.

Where his articles add or modify anything, this will be indicated. A fourth chapter will gather together and evaluate the reactions, both positive and negative to his view of consciousness. In a fifth chapter I will present my own conclusions about X's contribution, both its value and its limits. The thesis will conclude with an epilogue, summing up X's place in the history of reflection on human consciousness and suggesting some perspectives for future work in this field.

All of this means writing two or three relatively easy pages. More taxing reflection is needed to fashion and state a grid of questions that will serve to guide the critical investigation of the theme being handled.

(1) What sources did X draw on when elaborating his view of consciousness? Which authors does he quote or at least refer to, introducing them in support of his case or else critically rejecting them to establish his own position? Here one needs to distinguish. An explicit quotation carries more weight than a simple reference in a footnote, which could be merely 'decorative'. Sometimes statistics can prove illuminating: for instance, by establishing clearly the importance of some source: 'X quotes source Y fifteen times and refers to it twenty times.' Producing such statistics involves carefully differentiating, when one reads, between explicit quotations and mere references. Negative results may also be interesting. If X maintains total silence about some author or other source that one expects to find, what might we conclude? Is this a simple oversight or is the silence deliberate? If the latter, why might X have persistently avoided a source or another author that we would consider relevant to his project? Reflection on the sources used or not used, along with the authors with whom X engages in debate (or about whom he remains relentlessly silent), helps us to place and evaluate his views.

(2) We also need to ask ourselves: what question(s) does our author set out to answer? What audience does she address? The questions that drive our author, no less than the conclusions she reaches, shape in part what we judge X to have understood and achieved. Our judgments will likewise be affected by the audience she had or seems to have had in mind. Did she write for a strictly academic and specialised readership or for a broader, well educated public?

(3) Along with sources, questions, and audience, we should raise the question of presuppositions. What did X explicitly or implicitly presuppose when he wrote about human consciousness? Recognising not only the presuppositions that X frankly stated but also those he tacitly assumed (eg that serious reflection on consciousness can affect our view of moral behaviour) may yield precious insights into what we should make of X's mindset and arguments.

The specific presuppositions adopted vary widely from field to field. Obviously what dramatists, historians, philosophers, poets, political scientists, social scientists, theologians, and others might presuppose when they produce their works will differ greatly. Moreover, reflection on their presuppositions (along with a proper concern about their sources, questions, and audiences) should never excuse us from deep and prolonged attention to what they write. Sometimes research students and others will do anything rather than engage themselves seriously with the text(s). Nevertheless, some attention to presuppositions may prove illuminating.

In a variety of fields I always find it worthwhile asking: what counts as evil for these authors—for instance, for historians, theologians, and philosophers?

(1) Lord Acton (1834–1902), the Cambridge professor of modern history, famously stated: 'Power tends to corrupt and absolute power corrupts absolutely. Great men are almost always bad men.' This observation pointed to positions that Acton presupposed about what it was to be 'bad' or 'good'. Contemporary historians may be more reluctant to make moral judgments. Yet they too have their influential, often tacit, presuppositions about the characteristics and identity of good and evil.

(2) From what some theologians write it seems that major evil for them consists in false doctrine (or what they take to be false doctrine) rather than, for instance, mass starvation and genocidal massacres.

(3) As someone who began his academic life as a philosopher, I may be allowed to observe that for some philosophers evil takes the form of bad arguments. Whether we deal with historians, theologians, or philosophers, we may be enlightened by asking what primary shape evil takes for them.

Such then are some suggestions for drafting the introduction at the start of one's research. Of course, the text of the introduction will be revisited after the whole dissertation has been written. Yet a draft made right at the outset can clarify one's mind about the limits of the topic, the sources used, the methodology and direction adopted, and the questions that will be raised.

Whatever else happens, I think it is a mistake, after writing the entire thesis, to turn around and compose an introduction that summarises the findings of the thesis. If the text aims to spark and hold the interest of readers, it should ask questions rather than give answers and spell out conclusions.

What has been set out here about organising bibliographies and writing an introduction applies, I believe, not only to master's and doctoral dissertation but also to shorter papers to be written by undergraduates or by those following graduate courses and seminars.

Chapter Three
The Personal Touch

Before moving on to specific issues about research and writing, I want to make four suggestions that can be loosely gathered together as 'the personal touch'.

Introducing the Characters

Most, if not all, students appreciate that if their dissertation concerns a particular contribution of one particular author—for instance, her work on human consciousness—they need to begin with a more general, opening chapter. Who is this philosopher? Where did she grow up and study? Who were her principal teachers and, above all, who was her dissertation director? Can we spot any important influences that came into play when she developed her thinking on human consciousness? Finally, what academic posts did she hold?

This opening chapter should provide some overall indication of her contribution to philosophy as a teacher and writer. Her work on human consciousness belongs in the larger setting of her life, work, and publications. The reader expects some information about all this, before the thesis presses on in subsequent chapters to expound and evaluate the particular theme of her reflections on consciousness.

What some students may fail to recognise that, even though they do not limit their focus to one major figure, they would be advised to offer a little biographical information—perhaps only in footnote—about significant persons who turn up in course of their dissertations. I remember examining a thesis that compared and contrasted the contribution of four (somewhat minor) writers to a particular theological issue. Apart from it being clear that they all had written in French, the thesis offered no information whatsoever about where they had studied and taught and even whether they were still alive or were already dead. Had they lived and taught in France, Belgium, Switzerland, French Canada, or somewhere else? All four of them simply dropped 'from heaven' into the thesis. The student's silence about their identity and achievements seemed even more striking as he dedicated a chapter to each of them.

Meeting Your Subject

Some universities and other academic centres do not allow theses to be written on particular authors and public figures who are still alive. Other institutions allow for doctoral research on individuals who have made important contributions in their field, but have not yet died. In any case, many theses do not limit themselves to one specific living figure but range over the work of several contemporary writers.

Where one or more of the authors being studied are still living, my strong advice was always: 'please, send them a letter or an e-mail, explaining your research and interest in their work. Then phone their secretary, and ask for an interview.' Some students felt too embarrassed to do this. But those who followed the advice were invariably welcomed and gained further insight into the author(s) they were investigating. They could be reassured that they were not misinterpreting them, and could raise difficulties with the authors themselves.

My own PhD at the University of Cambridge compared and contrasted the work of four modern theologians on the theme of God's self-revelation. I corresponded with one of them, and visited two of the others. The immediate result was a sharper sense of what at least three of them had argued and a better grasp of the differences between them. A lasting result was a lifelong, fruitful friendship with one of them, Jürgen Moltmann (born 1926), an inspiring and ground-breaking German professor.

Further Networking

Some, perhaps only a few, of the master's and doctoral students that I knew and/or supervised over the years seemingly preferred to do their research alone in libraries, in archives, or at home. They all worked well but, I fear, lost the advantages that could have came from attending lectures and seminars that related to their research topics and from meeting leaders and research students in their field.

Some of the advantages that come from such 'networking' are quite blatant: immediate help with one's research project; information about possible grants that are available; contacts that can prove valuable in looking for jobs; meeting one or more professors who could turn out to be examiners of one's thesis. Apropos of the last advantage, it seems to me very useful, right from the beginning of one's research, to keep in mind those who in two or three years might become internal or external examiners of one's thesis. Personal contacts with such possible examiners never did anyone harm. Where such personal contact is difficult—for instance, because the academics in question teach at a university or college situated at a considerable distance—it could be advantageous to ensure that their work was acknowledged in one's thesis, even simply through one or two footnotes.

Such networking may extend also to other countries and other language areas. Where publications in one or more foreign languages are relevant for one's research, my advice is to learn those languages as soon as possible or, as the case may be, improve one's grasp of these relevant languages. It is fatally easy to postpone the hard work of language study. Where some other language is relevant or, more or less, essential to our research, the sooner we learn it the better.

Orderly Procedures

A proper self-love on the part of research students shows itself notably in their orderly procedures. They do help themselves along when they insist with themselves on being methodical, for instance, in gathering material for each chapter. In the past and, for some students, also today, every chapter had its own folder, in which they kept photocopied pages, personal notes, and downloaded material that seemed particularly relevant to that chapter. Nowadays many students practice that kind of orderliness in their computer files.

A chaos of disorderly notes and files can only stand in the way of producing a thesis. Why be disorderly when, with a little sense of discipline, a fruitful order of the raw material can facilitate swift progress in thinking through and writing the thesis?

Chapter Four
Writing Elegant Chapters, Paragraphs, and Footnotes

Each chapter and, for that matter, each paragraph of a thesis or of any scholarly book forms a distinct unit. Let me suggest some guidelines for composing chapters, paragraphs, and footnotes.

Composing Chapters

Normally chapters will be either descriptive or evaluative. The former kind of chapter describes the work of some author(s). It presents, for instance, what a particular philosopher says about her sources and her reasons for holding some views on human consciousness? Or else, for instance, it gathers and summarises the commentaries made by various authors on Milton's *Paradise Lost*. Or else, for instance, it provides an account, backed up with data, of what some political figure did in a particular period or in pursuit of a particular project.

Whatever the specific scope of the thesis, some chapters will gather, describe, and summarise what others have written or done. When composing such 'descriptive' chapters, students should avoid making judgments on the material. What they implicitly promise to do in such chapters is to set down faithfully and fairly what others have said and done. Evaluation should be kept to a minimum; it belongs to a later, separate chapter or chapters. One risks creating confusion if description and evaluation are mixed together.

If something puzzling or outrageous turns up in a descriptive chapter, the student might think of saying so in a footnote or perhaps in a passing aside. Describing what some person or persons wrote or did should be sharply differentiated from how I evaluate their words or actions.

Here clarity is everything. Readers want to know 'who is speaking': the author/public figure being studied or the writer of the dissertation. In Chapter 2, I mentioned a very good thesis that I once examined on the eschatological views of John Henry Newman. One blemish of that thesis, which was relatively easy to correct before its final approval, was an 'over-identification' of the student with Newman himself. In a few chapters the thesis ran on for pages without mentioning the name of Newman. It became somewhat difficult to know who was 'speaking': X or Newman himself. When pressed on this feature of his text, the student excused himself on the grounds that it would become 'tedious' or even 'boring' to introduce Newman's name too often. 'Clarity trumps any risk of becoming boring', I told him. 'Readers want to know whose voice they are listening to, even if it means saying four or five times on a given page "Newman", "he", or "our author"'.

Whether a chapter is descriptive or evaluative, it can often begin with questions. What reasons does X have for taking her position on human consciousness? Is she in debate with other philosophers in her first major work on consciousness? Such questions should follow closely what the title chosen for the chapter implies. After such preliminary questions, the chapter should proceed to offer the data that leads naturally to answers and, at the end of the chapter, to some conclusions.

Inevitably the conclusions reached at the end of each chapter will remain somewhat provisional until the whole dissertation is completed. Yet, in one chapter after another, they can and should be drawn on the basis of the data presented. That way of proceeding makes composing the final chapter much easier. It can gather together in a harmonious whole the provisional conclusions reached, chapter by chapter. That will involve a certain repetition in the closing chapter. But it will not be a repetition that jars. The impact will rather be like that of a great symphony which closes by evoking and bringing together themes that listeners have heard along the way.

Such a procedure avoids introducing any new data and any footnotes in the final chapter. What students state there has already been established, section by section over several hundred pages of their text. The final chapter may or probably should add, nevertheless, in-text references using parentheses: for instance, 'As we saw, X did not show her usual clarity when handling the objections brought by Y (Chapter 1, section 3 above)'. Here it seems superfluous to add 'see' and produce a longer in-text reference: '(see Chapter 1, section 3, above)'. But, if students choose that longer form, they should be consistent and use it everywhere.

Within chapters themselves, headings for various sections obviously help readers to follow the argument. But students should avoid excessive use of headings, subheadings, and numerical subdivisions. Some years ago such subdivisions plagued theses around the world: after 1.1, 1.2, 1.3, you met 2.1, 2.2, 2.3, and so forth, with some theses even pressing on to dazzle the reader with 1.1.1, 1.1.2, 1.1.3, and so on. Four or five numbered headings should be enough to indicate satisfactorily where a chapter is moving.

Such a modest use of headings requires, of course, that chapters maintain an appropriate, reasonable length, but not necessarily the same length. Chapters might run from around thirty to fifty pages. It is hard to justify chapters than continue for sixty pages or even much more. At the other end of the scale, chapters of only five or six pages look like odd fragments, and in any case hardly enjoy the chance of saying anything significant.

Occasionally I have read doctoral dissertations which ended with a very brief chapter. It always seemed strange that a text of three hundred pages or so had so little to say by way of conclusions. Perhaps the underlying problem was that the students had never been encouraged to reach provisional conclusions along the way, which they could then have woven together to form their final chapter.

Composing Paragraphs

In their own way, paragraphs also should not be either too long or too short. Paragraphs that continue for over a page are to be avoided. Paragraphs of only two or three lines can look bizarrely brief. The reader can be left wondering: was some distinct thought being developed in that paragraph? Or should it have been attached to the preceding paragraph or the following paragraph?

The run of thumb should be: one thought, one paragraph. Paragraphs may be seen as chapters in miniature, with a clear opening, a proper (limited) development, and a reasonable conclusion that brings everything coherently together. The worst paragraph that I ever read in a doctoral dissertation came right at the start. Thoughts galore jostled together in a way that communicated nothing with any clarity but merely left the examiners asking themselves: what is this thesis about? Where is it heading? It was only later that I realised that the student had put together in a kind of opening salvo the principal 'buzz' words of his thesis. Privately I pointed out to him how this paragraph of only twelve lines had jammed together nearly twenty, separate themes.

Normally paragraphs should begin several spaces from the margin, as I have been doing in this short guide. I recognise that another system starts paragraph flush with the margin. If students use that system, they need to leave an extra line between paragraphs.

Whether it happens right at the beginning or later on in a thesis and whatever different forms it takes, overloading paragraphs, chapters, and—one should add--footnotes sometimes results from students having gathered a great deal of material and then trying to cram into their text everything they have learned and discovered. This defect also shows up when bibliographies expand into endless lists of articles and books that only vaguely concern the research topic. Often it is the better students who suffer from this defect. They have unearthed a great deal of material and want to use it all now. They must learn that only what is clearly relevant deserves a place in their text. They can keep the rest of the material for later projects.[1]

---

1. Sometimes knowing too much leads students to indulge massive footnoting. Occasionally excessive footnotes can overshadow the text itself and take charge of the whole project.

Finally, let me add a warning about indented or block quotations: they are not equivalent to paragraphs but belong within paragraphs. An example can express what I have in mind. In a thesis that involved GK Chesterton (1874-1936) one might risk summing him up in a single paragraph:

'Chesterton published several fantastic novels, was a gifted poet, and enjoyed a genius for intuitively understanding great thinkers. He was also an extraordinary, eccentric character. As Roland Hill puts it:

> He was a true original of his generation in his intellectual and bodily dimensions. Wearing a huge cloak and a wide-brimmed hat, he carried a swordstick should he need to come to the aid of the weaker sex or fearlessly fight the wicked. The weaker sex, though, repeatedly saved him from himself, absent-minded as he was. "Am at Market Harborough, where ought I to be?" he famously cabled home while on a lecture tour. His wife merely cabled back "HOME" in order to dispatch him again to his proper destination [then follows a footnote to Hill's *A Time Out of Joint*].

To complete this sketch of Chesterton, one might add that he constantly spouted such aphorisms as: "If a thing is worth doing, it is worth doing badly."'

Here it would be a mistake to move several spaces in from the margin the sentence beginning with the words 'To complete this sketch'. Doing that would wrongly signal the start of a further paragraph, whereas the intention was to create only one paragraph. The indented quotation of seven lines from Hill's book belongs within a single paragraph, enclosed by four opening lines and three concluding lines.

In parenthesis let me insist on three things. First, indented quotations of less than four lines do not *look attractive*. They seem like odd fragments that break up a page. One should learn to insert short quotations within one's own text (and, of course, within quotation marks), so that the text can flow on smoothly. Second, indenting five or six spaces and adding a reference at the end shows quite clearly that the passage is a quotation. Hence, it is utterly superfluous either to add quotation marks or to set the passage in italics. In a kind of 'belt and braces' approach, students can be tempted to fall into either or even both of these mistakes. Third, in most cases you should prefer to paraphrase a source rather than quote it directly. Short quotations embedded in the text work best when they cite some particularly significant or happy expression; longer (indented) quotations are appropriate where you wish to analyse and comment in detail on the passage you cite.

Footnotes

In general, students should prefer footnotes to endnotes. Contemporary computers have taken away the problems about adjusting footnotes that plagued earlier generations of students who worked with manual and even electric typewriters. Footnotes obviously make life easier for readers; without turning pages, they can see at once what the author refers to.

Inconsistency in the style of footnotes and such vague references as 'pp 127ff.' raise questions for examiners about the scholarly precision of the dissertation.[2] When they notice at once, however, that the footnotes are precise and utterly consistent in style, this academically pleasing form will instinctively draw them to evaluate more favourably the content of the work.

Above I mentioned the danger of overloading footnotes with all manner of information. Students can sometimes avoid this by referring simply to a relevant entry in a contemporary encyclopedia that ends with an adequate and up to date bibliography. Occasionally a survey article recently published in a leading journal can perform the same function. In any case, footnotes should normally be lim-

---

2. Admittedly, p 145f. (= pp 145-6) is precise, but is better avoided.

ited to strictly relevant material – that is to say, sources on which you draw for significant facts and opinions.

When students refer to books or articles for the first time within a given chapter, they should provide full details: for instance, 'W. J. Featherby, "Revisiting Plato on the Good", *Adelaide Journal of Theology* 16 (2009), 231-66'. But, within the same chapter, any subsequent references should be abbreviated: 'Featherby, "Revisiting Plato", 45'.[3] In the case of books, the second reference within a chapter omits the date and place of publication, as well as the initials of the author, and uses only a short title. Thus the first reference would be: 'B. A. Levine, *Numbers 21-36* (New York: Doubleday, 2000), 18-20'. A subsequent reference would be simply: 'Levine, *Numbers*, 88'.

Nowadays most scholars avoid 'Featherby, op. cit.' (for '*opere citato*' or 'in the work cited/referred to above') or 'art. cit. (for *articulo citato* or 'in the article cited/referred to above'). Readers are expected to remember the work or article in question; if not, they have to thumb through earlier pages in the chapter. Such abbreviated references as 'Featherby, "Revisiting Plato", 45' make the reference perfectly clear. They also keep students well away from the ugly error of using 'op. cit.', when in fact the chapter has already cited two or even three articles by Featherby. In that case, readers are left wondering which article is being referred to.

Four Latin abbreviations continue to prove their worth and should be maintained. Where two or more consecutive footnotes refer to the same article by the same author, the second (or further consecutive) footnotes should simply run: 'Ibid 47' (preferable to 'Ibid.', *Ibid*, and 'Ibid, 47'). 'Ibid' (an abbreviation for the Latin *ibidem* [in the same place]) should not be used, however, where the previous footnote contains references to two or more articles or books, even though they may be works of the same author. To use 'Ibid' in such cases will create confusion for readers.

A second Latin abbreviation that remains useful is 'id' (for 'idem' or the same author). Where the writer is a woman, one should write 'ead' or give the term in full: 'eadem' (the same woman author). A

---

3. In footnotes the author's initials should appear before his surname (e.g. W. J. Featherby), but in the bibliography it should be the reverse (Featherby, W. J.).

footnote early in a chapter might include, for instance, two or more consecutive references to two or more articles by Featherby. The first time he should be named 'W. J. Featherby' or 'Walter J. Featherby'; to open the reference to the second article, 'id.' suffices. This means writing: 'W. J. Featherby, "Revisiting Plato on the Good", *Adelaide Journal of Philosophy*, 16 (2009), 231-66; id., "Vindicating Plato on the Good", ibid, 17 (2010), 15-30.'[4]

In footnotes or brackets 'e.g.' (= *exempli gratia*) replaces 'for example' and 'for instance'. While this Latin contraction for an English phrase is preferable in footnotes or brackets, the open or main text should give the phrase in full. Thus you write in the open text: 'Featherby reflected at length on Plato's notion of the good : for example, in "Revisiting Plato..."' Using a bracket, you would write: 'Featherby reflected at length on Plato's notion of the good (e.g. in "Revisiting Plato...")'.

A fourth and final Latin abbreviation that maintains its value is 'et al. (= et alii or and others)'. Some books have four or five editors; in such cases it is enough to write: 'A. N. Beale et al. (eds),...' Like 'idem', 'id.' and 'e.g.', 'et al.' is not underlined or italicised, even though it is an abbreviation of a foreign word.

Students should attend to the placing of footnotes (and intratextual references). Often enough, it should follow immediately after a quotation. But where an entire paragraph draws on some passage, let us say on an article from Featherby, and perhaps also quotes a phrase or a sentence from him (indicated by quotation marks), good practice would set the footnote (or intratextual reference) at the close of the paragraph. That shows that the entire paragraph refers to (and quotes from) the page or pages that are indicated.

A useful practice can come into play when citing articles (or at time specific chapters of a book), Where students refer to an article by Featherby but quote only one or two sentences, they certainly help readers when they construct the footnote as follows: 'W. J. Featherby, "Revisiting Plato on the Good", *Adelaide Journal of Theology*, 16 (2009), 231-66, at 250'. Readers know at once not only

---

4. On using 'ibid' and 'id', see *New Hart's Rules*, 320-1.

where to find the precise passage quoted or referred to but also the length of the article where they will find that passage.

A Certain Elegance

Whether writing footnotes, paragraphs, or entire chapters, students should 'watch their language' and aim for consistency and elegance.

As regards consistency, switching from the present to the past tense (or vice versa) should be avoided, at least within the same paragraph. If we spend a paragraph by saying, 'Gordon Brown normally failed to act decisively', we should not slip then into the present tense: 'But at the first meeting of his cabinet in 2010, he moves quickly…' The rule should be: within the same paragraph either use the present tense or use the past tense, but not a mixture.

As regards elegance, it becomes very tedious when every quotation is introduced by 'she says' or 'he emphasises'. There are numerous variations available for introducing quotations: for example, 'here he writes'; 'X goes on to explain'; 'Y puts it this way'; 'Z observes'. Many verbs can ring the changes on 'emphasise': affirm, argue, highlight, insist, maintain, stress, and so forth. When such variations do not come easily to mind, an up-to-date thesaurus will suggest various possibilities.

Perhaps more than ever, many students need to learn the art of writing well. Let me suggest *eleven ways* for doing that. First, a close reading of excellent authors and, especially, those not in one's own field of specialisation can do a great deal to improve one's style of writing. Keeping a 'commonplace book', in which we note down elegant or at least useful ways for expressing matters, remains a valuable practice. A well written thesis can be delight to read. The *form* of texts, including academic texts, is hardly less important than their *content*.

Second, with the advent of the internet and the key-pad of the mobile phone, the habit of letter writing seems to have declined around the globe. E-mails often massacre the correct standards of spelling, grammar, and punctuation. Those who persistently re-read and correct what they write in letters and/or e-mails will be rewarded by becoming better at producing correct and even elegant prose when they come to write their thesis. The classic adage 'practice makes perfect' applies eminently to the habit of correct and attractive writing.

Third, consistency plays its part towards ensuring elegance or at least avoiding ugly and unjustified variations. Total uniformity in spelling and in the use of lower (or upper) case throughout a thesis is, to put it mildly, desirable: thus 'toward' (rather than 'towards'); 'forever' or 'for ever' but not a mixture of both; 'lifestyle' rather than 'life-style'; 'judgment' or 'judgement' but not both; 'incarnation' and 'resurrection' rather than 'Incarnation' and 'Resurrection'. Right at the start of their work, students should decide about these and similar words. To remind themselves of the decisions they have made, they might think of making out a style sheet in alphabetical order and keeping it on their desk. A single sheet could have A to M in nine boxes on the front page and N to XYZ in six boxes on the back page. That might seem a homespun aid in these days of computers with more and more sophisticated programmes. But persistent experience has shown me how such a style sheet works toward securing a proper uniformity.[5]

Fourth, too many nouns can make one's style of writing unnecessarily ponderous. Verbs move things along briskly. Why write 'this is a manifestation of', when you could write 'this manifests'? Why write 'this was her understanding and interpretation of the new law', when you could write 'this was how she understood and interpreted the new law'? When correcting the chapters they submitted, over and over again I suggested to students that they should replace strings of nouns with some straightforward verbs. Excessive use of nouns produces prose that has to be characterised as heavy, even 'clunky'.

Fifth, research students (and other authors!) should carefully check what they write for any excessive use of the passive voice. Why write 'it will be seen' rather than 'we will see'? Why write 'it was noticed that X's behaviour had become erratic' rather than 'rela-

---

5. An appendix to this book offers an example of such a guide sheet.

tives and friends noticed that X's behaviour had become erratic'? Where possible and unless good reasons support using the passive, we should prefer the active voice.

Sixth, the English language provides us with various prepositions (and other possibilities) for avoiding a string of 'of-s'. We should not be happy about any sentence that begins like this: 'Such policies *of* strict treatment *of* asylum seekers *of* various nationalities…' Two of the three 'of-s' can disappear, as well as one noun: 'Such policies for treating strictly asylum seekers of various nationalities…' Quite often, as we see here, 'for' can happily replace an 'of'.

Seventh, inevitably students and other authors will use—and will have to use-- the verb 'to be'. But this does not excuse a lazy style that repeatedly fashions sentences with a noun followed by 'is' and then an adjective or another noun: for instance, 'a scrutiny of his close colleagues is pertinent to our understanding of this period of his political career'. Why not write: 'we need to scrutinise his close colleagues in order to understand this period of his political career'? I remember drawing a student's attention to the fact on a given page he had used 'is' in this fashion more than ten times. This can happen if we do not set ourselves to examine and justify any use we make of the verb 'to be'. The English language enjoys innumerable other verbs that can frequently and happily replace 'is' or 'are'.

Eighth, some guides to writing theses encourage students to avoid 'I' and 'we'. That can easily result in strange and obscure circumlocutions. One thesis I examined drew on some sociological research conducted in various parts of the UK. Over and over again the student wrote: 'research was made' or 'research was conducted'. I had to ask the student: 'did you or someone else do these pieces of research? And what's wrong with saying "when I finished this piece of research, I concluded…"?' Beyond question, too much use of 'I' or 'we' can create a sense of 'meism' and move the writer awkwardly into centre stage. But what harm is done by a straightforward use of 'I' and 'we' when that is appropriate and even necessary for the sake of clarity?

Ninth, foreign words (or at least those not yet sufficiently assimilated into English) should be underlined or put in italics: for instance, 'X writes here of the internal sacrifice (*sacrificium internum*)'. As we have seen repeatedly, the titles of books and journals should be underlined or put in italics. Otherwise, underlining and italics should be used sparingly. Some authors, like the late Pope John Paul II, have 'sinned' by too frequently introducing italics and/or underlining in order to emphasise some word or argument. Such repeated emphasis can make reading these pages of over-emphasised prose a breathless matter.

Tenth, a judicious use of 'road signs' can guide readers skillfully: in particular, by introducing 'first', 'second', 'third', and so forth. Incidentally, consistency requires that we do not switch back and forth – from 'first', 'secondly', 'third', 'fourthly', and so forth.

Eleventh, students should check their drafts to avoid 'jarring' repetitions of the same word occurring within one or two lines. It does not break any grammatical rules to write, for instance: 'In the 1950s the necessary development of postgraduate education in Australia was still a step away. A British option was still the only serious option for many Australians seeking higher degrees and an academic career.' The close repetition of 'was still' is not elegant. The second sentence could be rephrased: 'A British option remained the only serious option for many Australians...'

Having dedicated a few pages to elegance in writing, let me now turn to some typical mistakes that can easily alienate readers of theses.

Chapter Five
Words, Spelling, and Punctuation

Incorrect words, straight spelling mistakes, inferior or even false punctuation, and other such defects do not 'help the cause' of doctoral students and certainly reduce the value of the dissertations they produce.

Incorrect Words

In my experience, students need to watch carefully certain pairs of words that, while almost being letter for letter the same, have sharply different meanings: for instance, affect and effect; complement and compliment; plurality and pluralism; principal and principle.

(1) Readers will be startled to learn that 'the corrupt behaviour of some major cabinet ministers effected the morale of the prime minister'.

(2) A thesis I recently examined assured me that experts in religious studies detect a clear 'complimentarity' between Christian faith and some other faiths.

(3) This same thesis confused 'plurality', which generally carries the 'neutral' meaning of 'a large number of persons or things' (as in the United States when a candidate receives more votes than any other but not enough to enjoy an absolute majority) with 'pluralism'. Where 'plurality' indicates simply a 'fact', 'pluralism', as its suffix '-ism' clearly hints, refers to some theory, system, or even ideology that justifies the co-existence of two or more groups, principles, and so forth. In the area of religious studies, some

scholars endorse forms of 'pluralism', which understand and interpret various faiths as more or less equal ways to salvation.

(4) The officials who head some colleges or schools are often called the 'principals'; they would be astonished to find themselves named as the 'principles'. In this and other such cases (eg immanent and imminent), perusing the relevant entries in the *Oxford Dictionary of English*[1], the *New Oxford American Dictionary*,[2] or some other large, standard dictionary will help students appreciate differing meanings and nuances. Using language inaccurately does not, or at least should not, go down well with examiners.

Modern advertising constantly throws up examples of words being used falsely. I once spotted a store that proudly proclaimed, 'A thousand unique objects each week'. I have also read chapters in theses where students introduced, every now and then, 'unique'. 'Do you mean "the only one of its kind" or simply "very significant"?,' I used to ask.

Precise use of language—'watching your language', as we might name it—always enhances the value of texts and should tell in favour of their authors. A friend of mine, now retired after more than twenty years as a very successful editor of weekly journal, used to campaign against using 'practically' when his contributors meant 'almost' or 'virtually': for instance, 'the war lasted practically nine months'. 'Do you mean', he would ask, 'that the war lasted in a practical manner or in practice for nine months?' In the early twenty-first century, as the *Oxford Dictionary of English* acknowledges, 'practically' may *also* be now used in the sense of 'almost' or 'virtually'. But with gratitude I remember the lesson my friend constantly taught me in precise use of language.

One imprecision that occurs in dissertations involves a missing word, an 'also' omitted when using 'not only . . . but also'. It has surprised and saddened me to come across a few acceptable—I would not say, outstanding—authors who write 'not only . . . but' and never get around to adding the 'also'. Nevertheless, that did not stop me

---

1. *Oxford Dictionary of English*, (2nd edn; Oxford: Oxford University Press, 2005).
2. *New Oxford American Dictionary* (2nd edn; Oxford: Oxford University Press, 2005).

from correcting a dissertation I examined, which sometimes used 'not only . . . but also' and sometimes 'not only . . . but'. At least on the grounds of inconsistency, I could justify my correction.

A more blatant error turns up when students and others begin a sentence with 'On the other hand', but without having used an earlier sentence that began 'On the one hand'. This habit has been creeping into written English. One might argue that at the start of a sentence 'On the other hand' simply functions like 'However' or 'Nevertheless', and does not need an earlier, explicit 'On the one hand'. Maybe. Yet a certain lack of elegance remains. 'On the one hand' and 'on the other hand', in their own, contrasting way, belong together, as do 'not only' 'but also' in their 'conjunctive' way.

Misspellings and Variant Spellings

Spelling words wrongly should be avoided as much as possible.[3] Nowadays spell checks in computer programmes provide much help toward avoiding mistakes. But some errors can slip through undetected. We might type 'be' when we want to write 'he' and vice versa, 'casual' instead of 'causal', 'coma' instead of 'comma', 'form' instead of 'from', 'he' for 'the', 'martial' instead of 'marital', 'pubic' instead of 'public', or—worst of all-- 'it's' instead of 'its'. In this last case, many people continue to confuse the contraction for 'it is' and 'it has' (as in 'it's been a warm day') with the possessive 'its' (= belonging to it), as in 'I turned the suitcase on its side'. This confusion may be understandable, but remains completely out of place in scholarly writing.

Some forms of verbs may easily trigger misspellings. The past form of 'lead' is 'led', not 'lead'. It does not help the publicity for a conference to state in advertisements that 'it will be lead by Professor X'. The past for 'occur' is 'occurred', and the past for 'travel' is 'travelled'. Sometimes American usage normally prescribes no doubling of the consonant for certain verbs. Thus, 'worship' regularly

---

3. For help with spelling, see not only the dictionaries listed above but also *New Hart's Rules* (Oxford: Oxford University Press, 2005), 42–62, and Maurice Waite (ed.), *New Oxford Spelling Dictionary* (Oxford: Oxford University Press, 2005).

becomes 'worshiped' (and the protagonists of worship are 'worshipers'), whereas British English follows the spelling 'worshipped' and 'worshippers'. The participles and adjective follow suit: 'occurring', 'worshipping' (in the UK) and 'worshiping' in the USA. In this context I might also note the spelling of 'occurrence'; it is incorrect on both sides of the Atlantic to write 'occurence'.

Unlike the German language, English remains somewhat flexible about capitalisation. This flexibility affects, in particular, writing in the areas of biblical studies, history, and theology. In general, usage has reduced the number of required or preferable capitals. Nevertheless, it remains preferable to capitalise the Bible and the Scriptures, as well as three key events in the story of Christ: the Incarnation, the Crucifixion, and the Resurrection. At the start of their research and writing, students should create a style sheet showing their chosen capitals and then stick consistently to their choice. Here, as much as anywhere, strict consistency of treatment is indispensable.[4]

The spelling of names frequently becomes the occasion of mistakes. Sometimes these affect the first name. One journal managed to publish an article about Rudolf Otto (1869–1837) and, both in the title and throughout the article, call him 'Rudolph Otto'. The author of the piece and the editor of the journal missed the fact that Germans sometimes use the form 'Rudolf'. Over many years the same error afflicted the first name of Rudolf Bultmann (1884–1976). Joseph Ratzinger (born 1927), who became Pope Benedict XVI in 2005, at times appeared incorrectly as Josef Ratzinger. An older German scholar often suffered a similar fate: William Wrede (1856–1906) repeatedly appeared as 'Wilhelm Wrede'—presumably because writers did not know that Germans have occasionally used the English form of this first name.

Probably surnames or family names suffer more damage. There are the notoriously difficult names or at least names difficult for English-speakers: Edward Schillebeeckx (1914-2009), Friedrich Wilhelm Nietzsche (1844–1900), and Albert Schweitzer (1875–1965) to be distinguished from the less famous Eduard Schweizer

---

4. *New Hart's Rules*, 88–100.

(1913–2006). Sometimes the final 'n' gets omitted, as with Oscar Cullmann (1902–1999); sometimes a final 'n' gets added wrongly, as can happen to the Dutch historian of the Reformation, Heiko Oberman (1930–2001). On occasions an 's' fails to appear when students refer to Willi Marxsen (1919–1993). Over and over again, I found students ready to add an 'e' to the surname of Joseph A Fitzmyer (born 1920) and call him Fitzmeyer.

German umlauts at times do not make their expected appearance in such names as Hans Küng (born 1928), Ernst Käsemann (1906–1998), and the cities of Münster and Tübingen. Some Spanish names require the addition of a tilde, an accent at times placed over the Spanish ñ or over a Portuguese ã or õ. One might prefer not be bothered about umlauts, tildes, and further accents and diacritical marks, such as the circumflex in names like that of Georges Lemaître (1894–1966). But respect for reality and the kind of accuracy expected in any serious dissertation require otherwise.

Punctuation

Proper punctuation makes a text clear and its meaning quickly accessible. In a world of fallen standards, careful punctuation stands out by expressing genuine courtesy towards readers. They can see at a glance what writers want to say and how they want to connect or distinguish what they say.

When learning to insert appropriate—or, at the very least, correct—punctuation, students should realise that they have at their disposal not only quotation marks, commas, and full stops (or periods), but also brackets, semicolons, colons, dashes and hyphens, apostrophes, and further marks of punctuation. They also have at their disposal some excellent guides, like Lynne Truss, *New Hart's Rules*, and the *Oxford Dictionary of English*.[5] Here too one must aim at consistency, as well as correct usage.

---

5. Lynne Truss, *Eats, Shoots & Leaves. The Zero Tolerance Approach to Punctuation* (London: Profile Books, 2003); 'Punctuation', in *New Hart's Rules*, 63–87; and 'Punctuation', *Oxford Dictionary of English*, 2085–8.

(1) The demands of consistency, for example, will affect the positioning and use of *quotation marks*. Every thesis in the humanities will contain some, probably very many, quotations. The student should decide once and for all, right at the start of the thesis, whether to use single ('…') or double ("…") quotation marks (sometimes called inverted commas). This means using either the single or double system throughout, even when putting one or two words within quotation marks.

American English makes the positioning of closing quotation marks easy. They come after the punctuation of the sentence: for instance, "in a letter to X, Ludwig Wittgenstein urged him to 'attend to usage, not meaning.'" Or: "Attend to usage," Wittgenstein wrote, "not meaning." In British usage, however, where the punctuation is understood to belong to the sentence as a whole, the punctuation comes after the quotation mark: Wittgenstein urged him to 'attend to usage, not meaning'. Only where a quotation constitutes an entire sentence, the closing quotation mark would come after the final full stop. 'Attend to usage', Wittgenstein wrote, 'not meaning.'

Let us say the student adopts single quotation marks. This will mean double quotation marks within single quotation marks, whenever a quotation occurs within a quotation. For instance, Walter Featherby wrote: 'my aunt used to laugh at what she considered my pedantic behaviour. "Walter", she would ask, "must you be so eccentric?"'[6]

(2) In general, *brackets* provide explanations or additional material. The brackets that writers need most are round brackets or parentheses (…): 'during X's years as minister of education, principals (also called head teachers) found themselves increasingly frustrated by government policy'. Round brackets will be used when providing dates: for instance, Ludwig Wittgenstein (1889–1951). They occur when we cite sources in parenthesis: for example, (Featherby, 242). In such cases it is neater to position the full stop after the bracket: for instance, 'we shall see him [God] as he is' (1 John 3: 2).

---

6. On quotations, see *New Hart's Rules*, 152–66.

Occasionally we may need to insert brackets within brackets. Here it seems better practice to introduce square brackets within round brackets: 'during his years of office, X from time to time plagiarised speeches delivered by cabinet ministers in other parts of the world (eg in a speech in the lower house ["On curbing school principals"] made to the house on 26 May 1987).' Otherwise square brackets will be largely used to clarify or correct something in a quotation. Featherby wrote in his landmark article on Plato: 'this development in late fifth-century Greek history and thought led him [Plato] to concentrate further on moral issues'. When a quotation contains a straight grammatical or other error, we might want to show that it was found in the original source itself: 'in his autobiography Featherby argued that 'the democratic system of government and increased prosperity brings [*sic*!] widespread corruption' (Featherby, 377). In this case it can be sufficient to drop the sic (Latin for 'thus') and simply interject an exclamation mark: [!]. Rather than introducing an exclamation mark or a *sic*, better practice silently corrects such obvious errors as missing full stops or unclosed parentheses.

(3) *Commas* provide structure and prevent ambiguity by showing which words, phrases, and clauses belong closely together and which do not.[7] They express in writing the breaks or pauses that occur naturally in spoken English. In the case of long sentences, commas followed by a conjunction (e.g. 'and', 'but', and 'yet') signal the two parts of a sentence. They give readers a momentary 'breather' in the task of absorbing the text. In a long sentence an 'and', 'but', or 'yet' at the half way mark, preceded by a comma, provides this breathing space. Remember too that breaking up longer sentences into shorter ones could be clearer and would make less demand on the attention span of readers.

Writers often use commas to introduce quotations: for instance, Wittgenstein wrote to his friend, 'Are you attending to usage, rather than meaning?' It may be preferable or at least more emphatic to use a colon. Wittgenstein wrote to his friend: 'Are you attending to

---

7. On the use of commas, see Truss, *Eats, Shoots & Leaves*, 68–102; *New Hart's Rules*, 67–72; *Oxford Dictionary of English*, 2086.

usage, rather than meaning?' Incidentally, it is never correct to use semicolons to introduce quotations.

Commas are used in pairs to indicate 'asides', elements in a sentence that fall outside the central statement: for instance, 'all religion, of course, is the story of the human search for God.'

Most theses and essays in the humanities will involve providing some dates. American English usually inserts a comma: for example, July 27, 2009. In British English one conventionally omits any comma: 27 July 2009. Once again consistency requires strict adherence to one system or the other throughout our work.

Commas can be missing where they are needed, and present where they are not needed. When such adverbs as 'however', 'nevertheless', 'therefore', and 'moreover' introduce a sentence, they should be followed by a comma. In the case of 'however', the comma is vital if we want to distinguish between the use of 'however' as an adverb (eg 'However, I did not warm to him…') and its use as a conjunction ('However much I disliked him,…'). When 'however', 'nevertheless', and so forth do not occur right at the start of a sentence but a few words later, they should be surrounded by commas: for instance, 'I did not warm to him, however, even though he took me out to lunch'.

'However' and 'nevertheless' show that the way in which we speak should affect the punctuation we adopt. In spoken English, these two conjunctions begin a sentence emphatically; we want to add a statement that contrasts with or even seems to contradict what we have just said. This does not normally seem the case when 'but' and 'yet' open a sentence. Shorter than 'however' and 'nevertheless', these monosyllabic conjunctions allow the speaker to move seamlessly to what follows. Hence it seems hard to justify the way writers occasionally insert a comma after an opening 'But' or 'Yet'.

(4) Truss proves at her best in describing the appropriate ways of introducing *colons* and *semicolons*.[8] Theses and essays will employ colons to introduce quotations (and/or questions) and lists, especially long lists. In illustrating the former case, I used an example

---

8. Truss, *Eats, Shoots & Leaves*, 103–31; see also *New Hart's Rules*, 72–4.

that combined a quotation and a question introduced by a colon. Wittgenstein wrote to his friend: 'Are you attending to usage, rather than meaning?' Using a colon rather than a mere comma before a quotation, as in this example, gives more emphasis to the quoted matter. At times a thesis will include one or more questions introduced by a colon. 'This chapter will investigate the following issues: has the recent UK legislation affected the status of asylum seekers? Do these statutes differ from EEC legislation?' Incidentally, since the first question belongs within a sentence, it seems preferable not to capitalise the 'has'.

Lists may exemplify the use of both colons and semicolons. This chapter will summarise legislation that affects asylum seekers:
(1) recent UK legislation;
(2) secondary legislation found in the *Official Journal* of the European Union; and
(3) the international treaties and conventions that concern the protection of human rights. In this example, commas might replace the semicolons. But the semicolons effectively draw the reader's attention to three major divisions that the chapter will develop.

In general, semi-colons indicate divisions that call for something stronger than a comma but do not merit a full stop. A footnote illustrates this possibility: Featherby, 'Revisiting Plato on the Good', 235; see also *id 4*, 'Vindicating Plato on the Good', *Adelaide Journal of Philosophy*, 17 (2010): 15–30. Placing a full stop after '235' and then adding, 'See also…', separates items that belong naturally together: namely, the two articles by Featherby.

(5) As in one use of commas (see above), *dashes* signal an aside or parenthesis.[9] If we write, 'all religion—of course—is the story of the human search for God', we introduce a more emphatic break than a pair of commas provide. Students should avoid overusing the dash, rarely, if ever, allowing themselves more than two per page and certainly avoiding more than one use of dashes in a given sentence.

---

9. On dashes, see *New Hart's Rules*, 79–81; on hyphens, see ibid 52–7.

Hyphens link words in order to express a particular connection: for instance, the Asquith-Balfour relationship and numerous cases involving 'self' (e.g. 'self-revelation'). Hyphens also form such composite words as multi-ethnic and anti-Christian. Where prefixes previously required hyphens, this usage has quietly disappeared in such words as cooperate, neoclassical and reassignment. Usage has often dispensed with hyphens where they might be expected (eg lifestyle). Hyphens survive, however, in some words (eg co-producer) and in cases where we should avoid ambiguity: re-cover (put another cover on) and recover (return to normal or receive back) and re-sign (sign again) as distinguished from resign (give up one's office or post). Hyphens remain firmly in place to express a common second element in such expressions as two-, three-, and even fourfold.

(6) Apart from the hideous slip of the contraction 'it's instead of the possessive 'its', I found that most students use *apostrophes* correctly.[10] At times names ending in 's', like Simonds, proved troublesome. Thus I have read 'Justin Simond's views on the matter', instead of 'Justin Simonds's views on the matter'. 'Simond's' is simply incorrect. Most authorities agree that we add "s' when we pronounce—as we normally do—the resulting form with an extra '-s' in spoken English: as in 'Simonds's views on the matter' and 'Thomas's doubts'. Most avoid that extra '-s' for Jesus' and for such classical names as 'Mars'.

In a scholarly thesis or essay, it seems better to avoid such contractions that involve apostrophes as 'don't', 'doesn't', 'won't (wouldn't)', 'isn't', 'there's', and so forth. The formal nature of academic writing excludes the casual feel conveyed by such contractions.

---

10. On apostrophes, see *ibid*, 63–7, and Truss, *Eats, Shoots & Leaves*, 35–67.

Chapter Six
Some Don'ts, Do's, and Possibilities

My advice for those writing term papers and theses of various kinds includes a list of don'ts, do's, and possibilities drawn from decades of experience of supervising students from various parts of the world.

Some Don'ts

First of all, students should totally avoid any form of plagiarism or using the work of others without attributing it to them.[1] Plagiarism is always wrong, frequently betrays itself through a change of style, and in any case involves nowadays a much greater risk of being caught. Various computer programmes make it easier to detect.

At times sheer carelessness lets plagiarism creep in. Students transcribe passages from articles or books, without noting the source and using quotation marks. If they conscientiously note the source, they will be delivered from the danger of appropriating what others have written without acknowledging it.

Second, students who belong to the British language sector may be tempted to change the spelling when quoting American sources, and vice versa. Americans write 'behavior', 'color', 'worshipped', and so forth. Such quotations should not be 'emended' to produce 'behaviour', 'colour', 'worshiped', and so forth. Likewise, when citing the titles of books or articles written in foreign languages, students should be faithful to the original style. French and Italian titles, for instance, capitalise only the initial word. This convention should

---

1. On plagiarism and its evils, see Joseph Gibaldi, *MLA Handbook for Writers of Research Papers* (6th edn, New York: Modern Language Association of America, 2003), 66–78.

be followed, and students should refrain from bringing the titles of foreign publications into line with English usage.

A third piece of advice comes from the practice of some students who varied their methods of footnoting, moved ahead without checking the spelling of various words, and, in general left many items to be 'cleaned up at the end'. I always objected: 'Why do you waste your precious time?' If right from the outset they checked spelling, decided on the format for their references, settled the abbreviations they wished to use, and so forth, they could save days of work. In any case, if they allowed themselves to introduce errors and inconsistencies, they might not catch them all in a final 'clean-up' at the end.

Fourth, I could never understand those students who 'hoarded' their first, uncorrected chapters. If student and supervisor agree about changes, why bother to keep the original chapters? Doing that may well create confusion for oneself and one's supervisor. I still recall my earliest brush with the habit of 'hoarding'. Well into reading and correcting a chapter from a doctoral student, I realised that I had already made similar or even the same corrections and suggestions before. When the student came for supervision, he admitted that he had mistakenly printed out for me the original version of the chapter that he had submitted months earlier. 'But why keep the first, unrevised text?', I asked. 'How can it help you?'

Fifth, at times some projects and interests can distract research students from their central task. It may help their work to take on a little supervision of undergraduates. But they should not allow themselves to become overburdened by such teaching. They have three or so years to complete and receive their PhD. Let them put their heads down and finish their graduate studies, rather than let time slip away through work on other projects or, worse still, through cheerful social activities.

Sixth, where many students should be told, 'don't be distracted', a few need to told, 'don't become an unrealistic perfectionist'. A few students (and their supervisors) should be reminded that a PhD thesis is not the work of a lifetime. With regret and sorrow, I recall two cases of perfectionists. Before joining me for their doctoral research, both had completed excellent and very substantial MA dissertations (both several hundred pages long). Each of the two students had already efficiently gathered and presented the data at the heart of their research. To produce a doctoral thesis, they needed only to add a little more research and some further reflection on the criteria by which they should assess that data. One pressed ahead and wrote over a thousand pages. He continued to tinker with his work and would never agree to present and defend it, as he wanted his criteria to be utterly persuasive. The other student did not need to add many pages to his master's thesis. But he too could never be satisfied that he had made out his case perfectly and produced the definitive statement on his subject. Neither of them ever finished and defended their PhD dissertation; they were among the most intelligent students I have ever known.

Four Do's

After some 'don'ts', let me suggest, also out of a long experience, some 'do's' for those writing dissertations or even long essays. First, for better or worse, I have always preferred simple, straightforward names for files. Thus the files for a thesis on some of the philosophical issues addressed by Stephen T Davis could be entitled: DavisA, DavisB, DavisC, and so forth.

Second, some theses or essays involve frequent reference to organisations, publications, and realities of various kinds. Sometimes these bodies or realities already enjoy a conventional abbreviation or established acronym: for example, DNB (*Dictionary of National Biography*), FAO (Food and Agriculture Organisation), and TUC (Trades Union Congress). A theological thesis that discusses 'special divine actions' could well use the abbreviation of SDA(s), instead of repeating endlessly 'special divine action(s)'. In all cases, it is useful, even mandatory, to list alphabetically and at the beginning the abbreviations that will recur in the dissertation.[2]

---

2. On abbreviations and acronyms, see *New Hart's Rules* (Oxford: Oxford University Press, 2005), 166–78.

Third, a further 'do' concerns regulations for long essays, master's theses, and doctoral dissertations. Do please check those regulations, right at the start. Some universities, for instance, set limits to the length of PhD theses. Knowing that at the beginning of one's research should obviously guide the choice and treatment of one's topic. It also avoids the painful situation of finding one's thesis returned for shortening, even before any examiner has even received it.

A fourth and final 'do' recommends the addition of an index, at least an index of names. It does not take much time, and provides readers with an instant answer when they want to check how you have handled a particular scholar who could be relevant for your research. You may be writing a thesis on X. But what about Y, who also contributed to the same field as X? One of these 'relevant' scholars might also turn out to be the external examiner of your thesis. Back in Chapter 3, I suggested that personal networking could also include a willingness to introduce here and there in your thesis the work of scholars who might eventually be appointed external examiners. If that happens, they are quite likely to open the thesis at the index and see whether they were discussed in the thesis or at least received a mention. Such a listing in the index can turn out to be a first, important step in having them on your side.

One 'sin' that recurs in the indexes of many books takes the form of names followed by lengthy strings of page numbers. We should introduce subjects to break up such endless lists. This system of main entries and subentries provides the reader with effective help, and should always be introduced where seven or more page numbers follow a given entry.[3]

Some Possibilities

Students, without suffering from an extreme case of writer's block, may find difficulty in writing for the first time in their lives a substantial text. Some tactics can help them to engage with this diffi-

---

3. On indexing see *New Hart's Rules*, 355–70; for an excellent example of the way to set out entries and subentries, see ibid 397–417.

culty. Putting off the task of writing will not solve the problem. It is healthy to start writing as soon as possible. A chapter that calls for description rather than evaluation may be the place to start. Instead of planning to oneself, 'I will finish this chapter in three weeks', it could be easier to set shorter and more immediate targets: for instance, four pages a day. Some students I supervised encouraged themselves by doing their writing as if they were speaking to an intelligent friend who was sitting on the other side of their desk. Whatever the tactics that students adopt, they must avoid the situation of finding themselves, after two or three years of research, in front of a mountain of notes or dozens of computer files but without a single chapter written.

Second, *en route* to completing the thesis, students can try out some of their chapters by presenting them, in one guise or another, at seminars in their own department or elsewhere. Intelligent criticism and feedback will also come from fellow research students and from professors/lecturers other than their supervisor(s). At times students will have the chance of presenting some of their findings at conferences that involve faculty and students from other academic centres. Some students will profit from all the feedback available. It can bring to their notice sources that they might have missed; it can sharpen and even correct their judgments about the material they have assembled.

A further source of feedback might come from the editors of journals and their referees. I have known doctoral students who tried out some sections of their theses as articles in professional journals. Obviously, when submitting for publication in a journal what they intend to become a chapter of their thesis, they do not help their cause either by failing to follow scrupulously the house style of the journal (which may differ from the style adopted for the thesis) or by telling the editor of the journal, 'This article has been written as a chapter for my forthcoming thesis'. Let them simply submit the piece; if the editor and his/her associates judge it favourably, it will be published. They may also communicate some suggested corrections and changes before publishing it. Provided the article appears before the thesis is completed and submitted, some useful feedback may also come from readers of the journal.

In any case, publishing one or more chapters before completing the thesis will yield some powerful encouragement. Labouring through chapters three and four, the student knows: 'I have already published what will become chapter five. All I will need to do with that text is to adjust its opening and closing pages and fit it into the whole thesis.'

A third possibility, or even high probability, is that, earlier or later in their research work, students will experience some kind of crisis. In Chapter 1, I already touched on difficulties that can arise from one's supervisor and others. In the case of supervisors who take their time when reading chapters that students have submitted, I would tell students: 'Start working on the next chapter. Don't wait around for weeks or even longer until X gives you back your chapter. My guess is that he will not have very much to say anyway.' Sometimes the problem with a supervisor takes an extreme form, as when supervisors fall seriously ill or even die suddenly.

Personal sickness, family problems, an emotional crisis, and financial difficulties may also bring some painful stress. Or else students might become very bored with their topic. A severe loss of interest can descend on students, without their anticipating or causing this. In all cases, colleges and universities have officials whose job it is to counsel and support research students. They are there to help, and can often prove to be much more approachable than one's own supervisor, who may be part of the problem and with whom, in any case, it may be difficult to speak about the crisis.

Here I do not wish to exaggerate. Some students, perhaps a quarter, experience no crisis and not even a minor road block on their whole journey from choice of supervisor to successful defence of the thesis. But many do experience minor or even major crises. Being warned about this, from the very beginning, can take some pain out the crisis whenever it occurs and whatever form it takes.

Chapter Seven
Defending and Publishing the Thesis

This short guide to writing dissertations would remain incomplete, if it did not contain some advice about what happens at the end. Theses are presented, (usually) defended face-to-face, corrected, and (hopefully) published in part or in whole.

Submitting and Defending the Thesis

First of all, students should not allow mistakes to occur when they present their theses. Faculties, colleges, and universities have varying requirements about the binding and colour of theses and about the number of copies to be submitted. They also usually require students to submit an abstract that sums up the work being presented and perhaps some further forms. One should avoid causing irritating delays by failing to satisfy these ordinary formalities.

Students should also ensure that the title page, table of contents, acknowledgments, abbreviations (listed alphabetically), and lists of figures, illustrations, and maps are all in order: for instance, the titles of chapters in the table of contents should correspond exactly to the titles given at the start of each chapter. The table of contents, incidentally, will often be enriched by including (with precise accuracy) the headings used within chapters.

They should attend carefully to the title page; the more information provided there, the better. Let me explain through an example. The external examiner for the doctoral thesis submitted by a friend of mine managed to leave his copy of the thesis on the train when he alighted at Cambridge on the morning of the 'viva'. That copy of the text disappeared for ever. My young friend was naturally upset by the incident. What I could not say to him, however, was that he should have provided more contact information on the title page: his own postal and e-mail address, the name and address of his supervisor, and the name and address of the department for which he had written the thesis. (Some telephone numbers might also have been useful.) It did not seem enough for the title page to carry only the title of the thesis, his own name, the date of submission, and an indication that he had submitted the thesis at the University of Cambridge. Some more (contact) information could have led to the missing copy of his thesis being recovered.

Even after students have completed and submitted their term paper, long essay, MA dissertation, or PhD thesis, they may not have to face any 'viva', oral defence, or whatever a face-to-face encounter with examiners may be called. Some universities send papers and theses out for examination by one, two or three examiners, who simply send back their written reports. Even at the PhD level, a research student may never have to meet the examiners, but will only receive their reports.

More frequently, students at the master's level and, especially, at the doctoral level will meet an examining board at the end and may have met earlier with a committee when their thesis has taken more or less definitive shape. In such 'vivas' or meetings, students usually have to summarise their work and its conclusions and then face questions and comments from the board. In making their presentation, students should adhere strictly to the time allotted to them: fifteen or twenty minutes or whatever the time slot is. Nervousness or simply the desire to present all the valuable findings they have made can lead some students to go beyond, even well beyond, the allotted time. That may easily cause irritation, and hence become counter-productive.

What they should always include in their presentation are some words of thanks to their supervisor and any others who have provided significant help towards completing their project. At times it can also be worth mentioning any particular difficulties they faced in the course of their research. The thesis itself may contain no reference to such difficulties. Humanly speaking, it could be appropriate to let the members of the board know about them.

In responding to the questions and comments of the examiners, students should try as much as possible to avoid two extremes. On the one hand, some become overawed and agree too quickly with what examiners say. It often enough happens that an examiner misses some position developed in the thesis or misinterprets what students have written. In such cases, students should courteously explain and defend their text. Sometimes examiners raise an issue or put a question, not because they object to the thesis but precisely because they want to give the student a chance to clarify even further their methods, sources, and findings. Questions and 'objections' may be very friendly and offer students the chance to 'shine' at their 'viva'. They can miss this chance by nervously accepting everything an examiner is saying and failing to present their own views.

On the other hand, some students fail to understand questions that are put to them. If so, they should say so and ask the examiner to rephrase the question. At times, students set out to defend the indefensible: examiners may put their finger on a weak point–an issue that has not been well handled or sources that the thesis should have exploited. Students gain nothing by allowing themselves to become flustered and even annoyed, and by stubbornly insisting on what they have written.

All in all, the kind of good discussion one can hear at graduate seminars after someone has presented a paper offers an excellent model for a doctoral defence. It should be a learning experience for both students and examiners. Both 'sides' should go away with the feeling that they have profited from the exchanges.

Correcting the Thesis

In the aftermath of their doctoral 'viva', students will normally face the task of making some corrections in their written text. This may well be a requirement before a college or university definitively accepts the work. Sometimes the reports of examiners not only indicate obligatory corrections but also add some suggestions for improving the text. Students should be scrupulous about making the obligatory corrections. I have known a few cases where they carelessly failed to insert all such obligatory corrections and an examiner sent back the revised text and would not 'sign off' the thesis until all such corrections had been faithfully made. Obligatory means obligatory.

Furthermore, students should take seriously any suggestions for improving their text. As an academic, I have always been most grateful for any such suggestions made by my colleagues. Such peer help is an enormous boon. It is in that spirit that students should read, assess, and take advantage of all the suggestions made by examiners. I recall one external examiner who imposed very few obligatory corrections but added pages of helpful suggestions. When he received the revised text, he did 'sign it off' but indicated that he would not examine any further theses for the student's university. The student had completely ignored every suggestion made by the examiner, who played that role precisely because he was a world expert in the field.

Finally, students are advised to attend to corrections and revisions as soon as possible. Why delay matters? After all, a doctoral dissertation is a preparation for academic life and not life itself. The sooner students complete the whole process of being awarded a PhD, the better. But let me add a small proviso. I remember one doctoral defence that, like many such defences, took place shortly before the end of the academic year and the summer vacation. The student made the obligatory corrections and inserted many, if not all, of the suggestions made by examiners. Then he sent that final text by express delivery to the summer address (in a distant part of the world) of the examiner who, in this case, was solely responsible for 'signing off' the thesis. Yes, please be prompt. But please do not be unreasonably impatient. We can all wait until the end of the summer vacation.

Publishing the Thesis

Some, but far from all, colleges and universities require that a thesis be published, in part or in whole, before being finally accepted. Nowadays, if it has become more difficult to find a publisher ready to publish an entire doctoral thesis, matters have opened up on line. Electronic possibilities have, to some extent, replaced print opportunities. Accept the first publisher who comes along. Whatever the outlet, if a publisher expresses interest in publishing your thesis, accept this offer at once. Years ago, as the editor of a series, I offered to publish an excellent thesis. The student did not take up the offer but spent the next two years looking for another, presumably more prestigious publisher. Then he came back, hat in hand, to accept my original offer. Fortunately, I was still editor of the series

Nowadays drawing articles from the best chapters of the thesis normally remains the best option for students whose work has been accepted. Here I want to offer two pieces of advice. First, when shaping the chapter for submission, please follow the house-style of the journal you have in mind. Second, do not tell the editor that you are offering a chapter from your recently defended thesis. Saying that risks exposing your article to the fate of being summarily rejected. It is not dishonest to refrain from mentioning the origin of the article you are submitting.

Epilogue
On Supervising Theses

This epilogue could restate some of the suggestions already made: for instance, about the widespread need to lift the level of writing in students' theses. As one friend said to me, 'most theses are over-researched but under-written.' He emphasised the daily discipline of writing: 'Graham Greene set himself to write one thousand words a day. If he managed to reach that target by lunchtime, he stopped for the day.'

Another friend insisted: 'supervisors also have emotions. Students should remember the need to thank them—during the years of research and at the end.' A successful PhD should bring supervisors joy and congratulations. This friend added: 'even after the defence and publication of their theses, students should stay in touch with their supervisors. That kind of grateful, even lifelong relationship goes beyond the sheer need to have job recommendations from one's dissertation director.' This second friend, without intending to do so, encouraged me to add something in this epilogue on the role of those who supervise graduate research. To be sure, right from Chapter One this guide has also considered the role of supervisors but more should be said.

A Complex Task

Supervising research projects and theses, far from being an academic sideline, constitutes the most advanced level of teaching. Directing a PhD or even a Master's degree brings it own complex challenges that go beyond, often well beyond, the requirements for undergraduate teaching. It is a form of teaching that involves much time and energy, as well as serious reflection towards helping students design their research projects and carry them through to completion.

Yet, as far as my experience of universities and colleges around the world goes, dissertation directors and supervisors of research projects often simply take on the role without any precise preparation for this important, new role. They are thrown into the water or jump into it themselves, without any courses that might prepare them for the task. Perhaps some or even many academic institutions schedule seminars entitled 'Supervising Theses: What to do and what not to'. But I have never heard of such seminars, let alone had the chance of participating in them.

In what follows I will share some suggestions about supervising research, which apply primarily to the case of PhD and master's dissertations. But the advice and principles may also apply, with necessary adjustments, to directing research papers at the honors level in undergraduate programmes. In all cases the enthusiastic support and availability of the supervisor are essential for a happy and successful working relationship with students. This involves, in particular, scheduling regular meetings with them. Without such meetings taking place once a fortnight or at least once a month, students can feel isolated and their research can take head down false paths or even grind to a halt. Constant access to an encouraging and well informed director can not only save time but also work wonders in bringing research to a successful conclusion.

Four Suggestions

First, the initial meetings with a student may call for some time to be spent on clarifying the research project. Admittedly some students arrive with a thesis proposal, even a detailed one, which looks workable and promising. But often proposals may be too large and not precisely defined. Some questions from the supervisor can help to give the proposal a sharper focus. Such a sharper focus may emerge, to be sure, only in the course of the research. Good projects might turn out to take a somewhat different path and shape. But student and supervisor should work together, right at the outset, to give the project and the questions it involves some kind of sharp definition before examining in depth the data that could provide answers to these questions. In general, the rule of thumb should be to investigate thoroughly a specific issue rather than spread oneself too broadly.

Right from the beginning, a major part of the supervisor's role is to be a good sounding board, someone who listens carefully to what the student proposes and then raises pertinent and positive questions. The supervisor should be flexible enough to entertain projects that enjoy an unexpected novelty, and then should be adaptable enough to entertain new questions that might arise in the course of the research. But, initially, the supervisor plays the part of a well-informed, new friend who can help to give the thesis proposal a precise focus, direction, and structure.

Second, from their first contacts supervisors should show a strong concern that the students do a first-rate piece of research. But, at the same time, it is good to tell students that even the best PhDs do not normally produce the definitive word on their chosen topic. Their aim should be realistic: to complete a well researched and well written dissertation that has trained them in the practice of professional research, that deserves to be accepted by their examiners, and that will launch them into their academic career. In Chapter 6 above, I spoke of the need for students to be realistic and not succumb to the 'perfectionist' temptation. Supervisors also have their responsibility in helping students to appreciate that a dissertation, while requiring serious and persistent commitment, should not be allowed to become 'the work of a lifetime'. Rather they should see the dissertation as a major qualification that admits them into the academic guild.

Third, from day one it seems vital to initiate a warm rapport with students. In entering a programme with a view to a Master's or a PhD thesis, for the first time in their lives they take on a scale of research that goes beyond anything they have previously tackled. They can easily feel isolated and alarmed at the step they have made.

A supportive supervisor can help them to appreciate that their graduate research initiates them into a social process, in which other faculty members will also be available for consultation and suggestions. Networking with other students can also provide them with mutual support.

Supervisors, right from the outset, can do so much to facilitate and quietly improve their students' research. Encouraging them to read well written books, which might well be studies in other areas, can inspire a better quality of writing. Supervisors will often know about grants and other forms of funding, including subsidies to attend conferences and may even be in a position to secure an office for a research student. Providing such help establishes a warm rapport between supervisors and students and can do a great deal to launch the whole research projects. Where supervisors also make it clear that they wish to share in and learn from the research, they supply further motivation and encouragement to their students. That is after all the ideal that should guide doctoral research--as a shared intellectual pursuit in which both supervisors and students gain new knowledge and fresh perspectives.

Fourth, once the project gets underway, supervisors can facilitate its progress with constructive and prompt feedback. Few things can be more discouraging for students than waiting even months for their supervisors to read the latest chapter(s) they have submitted. Few things convey better to students a sense of their growing achievement than quick and detailed responses that include praise for what has been well done, along with suggestions for various improvements that are needed.

Examinations and their Aftermath

Supervisors normally have the chance to suggest, in consultation with other faculty members, the names of those who could be invited to examine their students' dissertations. It can forestall unnecessary worry if they do so *after* having consulted the students themselves. Students around the world pass on stories about strange and negative examiners who reject perfectly good theses. Being consulted and informed about what is happening works wonders in preventing the onset of anxiety.

Supervisors rightly propose examiners who are recognised experts in the field, whose judgment carries weight in the wider academic community and whose comments, questions and criticisms can make the viva a learning experience not only for the student but also for all present. Calling on such examiners could also provide useful contacts not only for students but also for the department or faculty itself. Intelligent and fruitful examining of doctoral and master's theses serves the cause of a wider networking between academic centres.

Almost always, examiners will recommend or even impose some corrections and even the rewriting of sections of a thesis. Supervisors should encourage students to do that work as soon as possible. They can also play a key role in helping students to publish the dissertation in whole or in part. Even if a thesis cannot be converted into a book, it normally supplies material for papers to be delivered at conferences and articles to be published in journals. All of that dissemination works to establish the names of their students as experts in various areas. Their supervisors are in a position to offer enlightened advice on how to go about publishing and presenting to a wider public the findings of their theses.

What I have been proposing about supervising theses presupposes a 'happy' conclusion. Yet one should not ignore the situation of those students who, after a year or more, abandon their research project. A personal crisis in their lives, lack of funding, and other factors, which may include an honest recognition that they have misjudged their capacities and should drop their aspiration to become academics, can trigger such a 'drop out'. Whatever the reasons, supervisors and students should arrange a final meeting and experience a sense of proper closure. It does no good on either side when students drift away or are allowed to drift away, without anything being said between them and their supervisors to conclude the relationship.

Finally, supervising a thesis to a successful conclusion initiates a relationship that can last for a lifetime. At least for the first few years after completing the project, many students stay in contact with their supervisors—for advice, help towards publication, and support when they apply for positions. Being a committed supervisor calls for such continuing interest in and support for the careers of their ex-students. On their side, former students often show their gratitude for the valuable supervision they have received—not least by organising and/or contributing to occasions and publications that celebrate milestones in the lives of their ex-supervisors. Few academic gifts can match the joy of finding that some former doctoral students have joined forces to produce a *Festschrift* for one's seventieth birthday or another major landmark in life's journey.

Select Bibliography

Austin, Tim (ed), *The 'Times' Guide to English Style and Usage* (London: Times Books, 1999).
Booth, Wayne C, Gregory G Colomb, and Joseph M Williams, *The Craft of Research* (3rd edn; Chicago: Chicago University Press, 2008).
Burchfield, RW (ed), *The New Fowler's Modern English Usage* (3rd edn; Oxford: Oxford University Press, 1998).
The Chicago Manual of Style (15th edn; Chicago: Chicago University Press, 2003).
Fink, Arlene, *Conducting Research Literature Reviews: From the Internet to Paper* (Thousand Oaks, Calif: Sage Publications, 2005).
Gibaldi, Joseph, *MLA Handbook for Writers of Research Papers* (6th edn; New York: Modern Language Association of America, 2003).
Lee, Raymond M, *Doing Research on Sensitive Topics* (Newbury Park/London: Sage Publications, 1993).
Levine, S Joseph, *Writing and Publishing*, University of Michigan dissertation service on line.
New Hart's Rules: The Handbook of Style for Writers and Editors (Oxford: Oxford University Press, 2005).
New Oxford Dictionary for Writers and Editors (Oxford: Oxford University Press, 2005).
The Online Writing Laboratory (OWL) at Purdue University, Indiana.
Turabian, Kate L, *A Manual for Writers of Term Papers, Theses, and Dissertations* (6th edn; Chicago: Chicago University Press, 1996).
Truss, Lynne, *Eats, Shoots & Leaves: The Zero Tolerance Approach to Punctuation* (London: Profile Books, 2003).

A Guide Sheet

A	B	C
D	E	F
G	H	I J
K	L	M

N	O	P Q
R	S	T
U V	W	X Y Z

Index

Acton, Lord	28		Greene, G	21, 69
Alonso Schökel, L	23		Harnack, A von	23
Asquith, HH	56		Hesse, H	11
Austin, T	75		Hill, R	39
Balfour, AJ	56		Hume, D	14
Balthasar, HU von	23		Hünermann, P	21
Beale, AN	42		Hunt, A	4
Begley, J	4		Käsemann, E	51
Booth, WC	75		Kendall, D	21, 25
Borchert, DM	12n.		Küng, H	51
Bowra, CM	20		Lee, RM	75
Brown, G	43		Lemaître, G	51
Bultmann, R	20, 50		Lessing, D	11
Burchfield, RW	75		Levine, BA	25, 41
Chesterton, GK	39		Levine, SJ	75
Colomb, GG	75		Livingstone, EA	20
Connelly, S	4		Lubac, H de	23
Craig, E	12n.		Marxsen, W	51
Cross, FL	20n.		Milton, J	13, 35
Cullmann, O	51		Moltmann, J	32
Dante Alighieri	13		Murdoch, I	20
Davis, ST	21, 25, 59		Murray, G	20
Denniston, JD	21		Newman, JH	13, 36
Denzinger, H	21		Nietzsche, F	50
Eliot, TS	13		Oberman, H	51
Endo, S	13		O'Neill, E	13
Faulkner, W	13		Otto, R	50
Featherby, WJ	21, 24, 25, 41, 42, 52, 53, 55		Plato	41, 42, 53, 55
			Playoust, C	4
Fee, GD	21, 25		Rahner, K	20
Fink, A	75		Ratzinger, J	50
Fitzmyer, JA	51		Schillebeeckx, E	50
Gandhi, Mahatma	14		Schweitzer, A	50
Gibaldi, J	3, 57n., 75		Schweizer, E	50
Gladstone, W	14		Shakespeare, W	13, 14

Sherry, N	21
Simonds, J	56
Smith, M	4
Sun Yat-Sen	14
Tagore, R	13
Teilhard de Chardin, P	23
Truss, L	51, 53, 54, 56n., 75
Turabian, K	4, 75
Uren, W	4
Waite, M	49n.
Washington, G	14
White, P	11
Williams, JM	75
Williams, T	13
Wilson, AN	20
Wittgenstein, L	52, 53, 55
Wrede, W	50
Wright, NT	20
Yeats, WB	14

Lightning Source UK Ltd.
Milton Keynes UK
UKHW010006090922
408557UK00003B/486